But God...

My Story

by Kathy Eudy

But God... My Story
By Kathy Eudy
Copyright 2021. All rights reserved.

No portion of this book may be reproduced in any form without permission from the publisher, except as permitted by U.S. copyright law. For permissions contact: RHEMA Publishing House, PO Box 1244 McKinney, TX 75070

Unless otherwise indicated, all Scripture quotations are taken from the Holy Bible, New Living Translation, copyright © 1996, 2004, 2007 by Tyndale House Foundation. Used by permission of Tyndale House Publishers, Inc., Carol Stream, IL 60188. All rights reserved.

Scripture quotations marked TPT are from The Passion Translation®. Copyright © 2017, 2018 by Passion & Fire Ministries, Inc. Used by permission. All rights reserved. ThePassionTranslation.com.

Scriptures marked KJV are taken from the KING JAMES VERSION (KJV): KING JAMES VERSION, public domain.

Scripture taken from The Message. Copyright © 1993, 1994, 1995, 1996, 2000, 2001, 2002. Used by permission of NavPress Publishing Group.

ISBN: 978-1-7330710-8-6 paperback
ISBN: 978-1-7330710-9-3 ebook

Interior formatting: Lee Desmond
Cover design: Kathy Gifford

Dedication

Garry, you are the love of my life. I've loved you since that day you looked down at me with those beautiful blue eyes and called me little Scog. I will forever be grateful that God gave you to me. You, more than any human, have taught me how to love God and others. Having you as my first love is special, but having you as my last is beyond perfect. I love you, *mi amor*, and I always will.

Christen, Grant, and Greg, you are my three greatest, most beautiful gifts from God. I'm not only proud of you for what you've accomplished in life, but mostly I'm proud of who you are—lovers of God, your families, and others. Always remember that I will forever love you, your spouses, and your children more than life itself.

Kayla, Morgan, Andrew, Samuel, Michael, Daniel, Jared, and Kaylee—being your Tita has been one of the greatest joys of my life. When you struggle or go through difficult times, I imagine myself placing you into the precious open arms of Jesus, knowing that He loves you even more than I do. He has the perfect plan for your life. I pray you will always follow Him and share His love wherever He takes you. As for me, I will always cherish my memories with you, the laughs we've shared, the fun we've had, the hugs you've given me, and the love I feel from you. All of you are my favorites! Never, ever forget that there's nothing like Tita love.

Ann Marie, you are my favorite sister! Thank you for "getting me" and understanding who I am and how I got here. Thank you for putting up with my bratty self as a child and allowing me to become one of your best friends today. We've come a long way, baby. I love you so much.

iv

Acknowledgments

Thank you to all of you who went before us, worked beside us, traveled with us, encouraged us, prayed for us, and loved us during our journey with God. I love you all. I can't imagine my life without you.

Kathy Owen Gifford, thank you for being my book's first reader, editor, designer, and new best friend! God knew I needed you, and He sent you to me. I love you mucho!

We always thank God for all of you and continually mention you in our prayers. We remember before our God and Father your work produced by Faith, your labor prompted by Love, and your endurance inspired by Hope in our Lord Jesus Christ.

1 Thessalonians 1:2-3

Foreword

Don't ever let anyone tell you that God doesn't exist. Don't ever believe that life ends at death. The truth of God's Word, all of creation, and the evidence of changed lives scream the Truth. He is an Amazing, Caring, Faithful Creator and Loving God. His Heart is full of Grace, Mercy, and Forgiveness.

Does this Truth mean we understand God's ways or everything that happens to us in life? No, it definitely does not. But it does mean that when we're discouraged, afraid, confused, or just in a bad place emotionally, physically, or spiritually, He is there, passionately pursuing us. We either choose to follow Him or decide not to.

Whoever you are, please know that God loves you with an Eternal and All-Consuming Love. He sees you. He knows you. He has a perfect plan for your life. It begins when you realize that He wants a relationship with you and lovingly sent His Son Jesus to you so you could know Him. Jesus came into a dark, dark world and became the Light of our world.

When I think about His miraculous birth, I feel Peace. When I think about His beautiful Life, I feel Comfort. When I think about His sacrificial death for me, I feel so Loved. When I think about His resurrection, I feel overwhelming Joy. And when I think about His coming again, I feel Hope—if I die before He comes back, I will experience—face to face—His sweet Presence.

This book is about my incredible journey with God. Even as a child, I thought I had my life all figured out. I was all about doing my own thing, or what I thought was God's will for my life. *But God* not only had a better plan for me; He had the perfect Plan. That doesn't mean I'm perfect or special; I certainly am not. I didn't come from a perfect family. I didn't marry a perfect man. I don't have perfect children or grandchildren. In our genealogy, we've dealt with drunkenness, drugs, and pornography. Some of us have had struggles with feelings of rejection, deep-rooted insecurities, and sexual identity. Thankfully, through it all, we've experienced God's Amazing Grace and Unconditional Love. I realize, truly, that I'm just a perfect Nobody. I also know that when I've chosen to follow God and be obedient to His will, He has guided me and been with me every step of the way, even when I didn't feel His Presence. And, most importantly, He has allowed me to watch Him work. Many times, I didn't realize He was working—*But God* never failed to show me that He has always been at work in my life. Watching Him work has been the single most amazing blessing I could've ever experienced. I can't even begin to imagine my life without Him. I hope my story points you to Him.

And I am convinced that nothing can ever separate us from God's love. Neither death nor life, neither angels nor demons, neither our fears for today nor our worries about tomorrow—not even the powers of hell can separate us from God's love. No power in the sky above or in the earth below—indeed, nothing in all creation will ever be able to separate us from the love of God that is revealed in Christ Jesus our Lord.

Romans 8:38-39

Contents

Dedication iii

Acknowledgments v

Foreword vi

Chapter 1 1

Chapter 2 6

Chapter 3 8

Chapter 4 10

Chapter 5 12

Chapter 6 16

Chapter 7 17

Chapter 8 20

Chapter 9 22

Chapter 10 25

Chapter 11 28

Chapter 12 32

Chapter 13 34

Chapter 14 36

Chapter 15 39

Chapter 16 40

Chapter 17 42

Chapter 18 45

Chapter 19 48

Chapter 20 50

Chapter 21 53

Chapter 22 55

Chapter 23 57

Chapter 24 60

Chapter 25 62

Chapter 26 65

Chapter 27 68

Chapter 28 71

Chapter 29 73

Chapter 30 75

Chapter 31 78

Chapter 32 80

Chapter 33 82

Chapter 34 86

Chapter 35 89

Chapter 36 92

Chapter 37 96

Chapter 38 99

Chapter 39 105

Chapter 40 108

Chapter 41 111

Chapter 42 114

Chapter 43 117

Chapter 44 119

Chapter 45 122

Chapter 46 125

Chapter 47 128

Chapter 48 131

Chapter 49 133

Chapter 50 138

Chapter 51 140

Chapter 52 144

Chapter 53 146

Chapter 54 149

Chapter 55 152

Chapter 56 154

Addendum 158

x

Chapter 1

I can truthfully say Garry and I could have never imagined the life that God had planned for us when we got married over 50 years ago at Shades Mountain Baptist Church in Birmingham, Alabama. For our wedding, a song had been written for us. As we walked down the aisle and out of the church, *We'll Walk with God from This Day On* was being sung. All we really knew was that we were madly in love and just wanted to be together. We had met at vacation Bible school at Boyles Baptist Church in Tarrant. He had gone there to meet the girls, and he met me. I was 13; he was 16. We didn't realize it then, but we were two immature, hurting, needy, and totally dysfunctional kids.

My parents were good people, but I know they were emotionally scarred. My mother had been raped by her alcoholic daddy when she was five years old. My daddy had been raised by what I call "emotionally crippled" parents. They never touched or expressed feelings of acceptance or love. Daddy parented the way he was parented.

I remember stories about me being a brat as a kid. I would hold my breath until I passed out if I didn't get my way. I even had a screaming fit on the streets of Birmingham because my mother bought me some ugly brown shoes instead of pretty red ones. I was taken to church every time the doors were open, but I remember it being mostly about what you didn't do, instead of having a loving relationship with Jesus. You didn't "cuss, drink, dance, smoke or chew, and you didn't hang out with those that do!" I knew without a doubt, though, that when I asked Jesus to come into my life at age eight, He did.

That decision, however, did not mean I was a perfect child. I mean, I sang duets with my friend Lois at Sunday night church, but I might have had a little sneaky streak in me. My friend Kay and I snuck into our 5th grade classroom one morning and spread a couple of bags of manure into inconspicuous places. Our teacher was always complaining about smelling our tennis shoes; the smell that afternoon, however, didn't come from our shoes (we even put manure into her desk). Kay and I also snuck out at midnight from a sleepover at her house and made a visit to Garry's house about two miles away. Garry couldn't believe it when we tapped on his window and woke him up—he thought we were crazy. We *knew* we were.

My older brother Jim and I were the troublemakers in our family. He and I tortured our older sister Ann Marie. When Jim and I wouldn't do what she told us to do, she would call our mama at work. If she had to come home, my brother and I got into big trouble. We weren't smart like Garry and his younger brother

Jack; they would pack their jeans with newspaper if they knew they were getting a spanking when their daddy got home .

Really, I had a pretty normal childhood. I skated a lot, practiced the piano, rode my bicycle, and played touch football with the neighborhood kids. There were times, though, that I feel I will never get over. Often, my mama would take me to her aunt and uncle's apartment. I couldn't believe the smell each time we went in; it was a mixture of pee and alcohol. They would be in their beds, and my sweet mama would get them out of bed, clean them up, and wash the bed linens. She always talked with them about Jesus, and she begged them to stop drinking. Sadly, they never did. Mama had another uncle who died, drunk, in the streets of Birmingham. Daddy had to go get his body and bury him because there was no one else who cared.

Garry's parents loved him very much, but they didn't take him to church. His daddy, who was a WWII Combat Veteran, abused alcohol. Throughout Garry's childhood and youth, his daddy's drinking caused serious problems at home; and his granddaddy was known as the "town drunk." He remembers as a kid going with his uncle to pick up his granddaddy on Friday nights. He would get paid and then get drunk. Years later, his granddaddy got a visit from our pastor, and his life was changed forever. But at the time, Garry was not influenced by that decision.

Garry grew up playing all the sports, and he was good. He went to church occasionally and even joined a church, but he didn't really know the Lord. However, thanks to my church's sports programs (basketball and softball), Garry got involved, and we could be together. I loved sitting next to his sweaty body on the rides home from the games. I had never seen anybody catch a ball and then turn a flip quite like he did out in left field. He had a hard time letting go of his anger, though. At one of the basketball games, he totally tackled a guy from the opposing team and beat him up for making some inappropriate remark to me. Oh, but I loved him for doing that! A guy who will fight for you is hard to find.

Garry's teenage years were filled with bad choices, bad habits, and rebellion. When someone would ask him where he was going, he would laugh and say, "To hell, if I don't change." I probably shouldn't have ever dated him, but I really liked him and loved being with him. I was also impressed with his work ethic. Because of a knee injury, he quit playing football and started working at a grocery store when he was 16. I would go to the grocery store with my mama so I could see him. I would tell her to go through his line so he could bag and take out our groceries. Then I'd tell her to give him a big tip!

I could tell that Garry had a good heart, but he was indeed a challenge. One night when we had just begun going out together, he told my mama we were going downtown to the Alabama Theatre to see a movie—but when I got into his car, he told me we were going to the drive-in theatre instead. He then introduced me to the couple in the back seat; they were double-dating with us because I was not allowed to go out alone with a boy. I greeted them but never saw them again that night because they disappeared into the back seat and never came up for air!

On the way, I told Garry that I needed to let my mama know where we were going, so he took me to a phone booth in town, and I gave her a call. She told me, "Okay, just be nice." She trusted me. Garry must've thought that was funny, because he chuckled when I told him what she said. When we got settled at the drive-in, he scooted over in his 1956 Chevy, put his arm around me, and tried to kiss me. But my mama told me to be nice, so I didn't let him— although Garry didn't stop trying.

I also remembered my brother's words to me: "I'd better not ever see your name and phone number written on the stall door of any boy's bathroom!" Finally, at intermission, he asked if I was mad at him. Of course, I wasn't mad at him; I just didn't think it was a good idea to "make out" at the drive-in. He looked down at me with those beautiful blue eyes shining in the light and said, "You're the nicest girl I've ever known." I think that was the moment I fell in love with him. And the kiss on my front porch that night was the sweetest kiss ever.

The bad boy in Garry didn't care much about his schoolwork; it just was not a priority for him. He would even skip classes at his high school and come see me at mine. And he wasn't planning on going to college. After all, his dream was to join the Army after high school and be an Army Ranger like his daddy.

But God, ...pursues us with an everlasting love.

Jeremiah 31:3

God had a different plan for his life. He wanted Garry in His Army. I'll never forget one August night before his senior year when he literally ran from the back of the church down the aisle and gave his life to Jesus. The change in Garry's life was unbelievable. God took his broken life, forgave his sins, and gave him purpose and direction. Two years later, he felt God was calling him to preach. Not long after that, Boyles Baptist Church asked him to be their youth pastor. God began using him to influence people to give their lives to Jesus, including his sister Kathy and his brother Jack.

There's another piece to our story that is also quite incredible. When I was very young, God put in my heart a strong desire to marry a preacher. I just had no clue that when I met and fell in love with Garry, he would be the man who God would save, call to preach, gift, and give to me. *But God* knew, and He planned it. There was absolutely nothing special about us, but together, we were about to take an extraordinary walk with God.

"We'll walk with God from this day on. We'll talk with Him; He's on His throne. We'll walk with Him; we'll talk with Him from this day on."

Song written for our wedding, sung as we walked out together.

Take delight in the LORD, and he will give you your heart's desires. Commit everything you do to the LORD. Trust him, and he will help you.

Psalms 37:4-5

Chapter 2

We dated for over four years, but my parents were panic-stricken on the day Garry approached them to ask if we could get married. Even though he had proven himself to be responsible by working his way through Samford University and getting scholarships, he was not good enough to marry their spoiled daughter. My mama ran off into her bedroom crying. My daddy responded to Garry's, "Mr. Scogin, Kathy and I want to get married," with this: "Well, I think your 'want to' has outrun your 'able to.'" Alrighty then! So much for parental approval and consent.

That didn't scare Garry, though. Eventually, he bought me a ring, and we set the date. My parents still wanted us to wait until I finished college. My mama's exact words were, "I know you won't finish school. You'll get pregnant." All I had left to graduate was my senior year, and my response was, "Mama! I know what causes that, and it won't happen! I will finish!" So, the evening after the morning that Garry graduated from Samford, we got married. I was 19, and he was 22.

The next day we set off for New Orleans Baptist Theological Seminary. We had an old car, and we had a flat tire on the way. Garry bought us an ugly old trailer and put it on campus next to the railroad tracks in the back. The truth is that we were as poor as Job's house cat. Several things happened in those first months: Garry found a part-time job, I enrolled in Louisiana State University, New Orleans for a few required credits, and we both began classes. I got my first tick, my first case of ringworm, and, yes, I got pregnant. I'll admit that I was afraid to tell my mama. I had been pretty sick with morning sickness when she and my grandparents came to visit. She brought a cooler full of meat and other goodies to share with us. When she was unloading them, she saw my full freezer, and she turned to me and said, "Have you not been cooking?" "No, Mama, I've been sick." "Are you pregnant?" "Yes! But I don't know HOW it happened!" My Papaw spoke up and said, "El, I can

Our first Christmas

tell ye how it happened!" Mama was not amused and said, "You just wait till I see Garry Eudy!" "Well," I said, "It's not HIS fault either!"

Oh, yes! That surprise/blessing was the first of many in our married life. Christen was born 11 months, almost to the day, after we got married. She was the most beautiful and smartest baby I had ever seen. I was in love with her, and so was her daddy. He actually changed her first diaper because I didn't know how.

Oh, and two months before she was born, I graduated from The University of Alabama, and I even walked—I walked out the door of our parsonage in Gilbertown, Alabama, to our mailbox and unwrapped my diploma. I couldn't believe it, *But God* had been so good to me. At 20 years old, I was a mommy, a college graduate, and I was the pastor's wife at our first church, Chappell Hill Baptist.

You thrill me, LORD, with all you have done for me! I sing for joy because of what you have done.

Psalms 92:4

Chapter 3

I look back on those days and wonder how in the world we made it. On weekdays Garry attended seminary classes and worked in a men's clothing store while I taught school. Every weekend we traveled four hours to our church with our baby in the back seat in a port-a-crib. At that time, we knew literally nothing about parenting or pastoring. All we knew how to do was love. And our beautiful baby and those precious church members loved us back. It helped that Garry had such a passion for telling people about Jesus, and ministering to and visiting people in their homes. It also helped that our church members loved Christen like she was their own.

One of the most special times of our ministry happened at Chappell Hill. We had our first revival, and many people came to know Christ. On the last night, they were to be baptized. As our pastor, Garry stepped into the water and said, "I was baptized when I was nine years old when I joined a church, but I wasn't saved until I was 17. I need to get this right." So his friend, the pastor leading the revival, baptized him. Then Garry turned and baptized the others. I so loved him for that. He showed no pretense or pride, just humility and obedience.

...for God opposes the proud but gives grace to the humble.

1 Peter 5:5

There were times at Chappell Hill that were not so special. One night we heard a noise outside our house next to the church. Our drunk neighbor, who was wielding a shotgun, was calling Garry to go outside and fight him. I'm sure Garry could've whipped him, but he chose to talk him down and told him to go home. The neighbor was upset because he thought our youth group had been making too much noise with their music. He finally left, and we more or less rested easy that night.

On another occasion, Garry went to visit an older church member down the road. He knocked, and her daughter came to the door with her shotgun. Garry jokingly said, "Well, hey there! You're not going to shoot the preacher, are you?" She looked at him intently and said, "Ell, I've yet tah shoot my first un." Translated, that's "Well, I haven't shot one yet!" Garry didn't stay very long there.

It was there that I learned that not all church members are nice. There was one lady who had been a thorn in the flesh for many pastors before Garry. She was everything I didn't want to be when I grew up. She was totally frustrated because she—in all of her drama—couldn't run him off or tell him what to do. *But God* did not honor her mean spirit, and He was not ready for us to leave until after our second biggest blessing arrived.

Chapter 4

When Christen was 18 months old, I found myself expecting again. My trips to New Orleans stopped, and Christen and I stayed all week in Gilbertown, waiting for Garry to come home on the weekends. I had some beautiful friends there, and they took good care of me. When I was in my sixth month, one of my friends told me I looked like I was carrying twins. On my next visit to the doctor, he checked me for two heartbeats. "No," he said, "You're having one big baby, and the baby will be born earlier than we thought." I had no reason not to believe him.

About a month before our baby was due, Garry's granddaddy passed away, and we made a trip to Birmingham for the funeral. After the funeral, Garry's daddy told us he was leaving for a visit with his cousins. Garry knew that he was going there to drink with them, and he tried to stop him. When he returned, we were able to have a serious talk with him. We told him that we just could not allow our children to be around him while he was drinking. If he wanted us to bring them for a visit, he would have to stop abusing alcohol. We had no idea how that would work out, *But God* worked it out! As far as we know, he never drank again, and he became a gentle, loving, fun Papaw to his grandchildren. They loved him very much.

What's happening?!

A couple of weeks later, I went into labor. And, sure enough, it was three weeks earlier than my due date. We lived 60 miles from the hospital in Meridian, Mississippi, and Garry broke the law all the way, going 80 miles per hour on the curvy roads to the hospital. We arrived at midnight, and at 2:00 a.m., our son Grant was born. He was precious, but oh, so little. The doctor stood over me and said, "You look too big not to have another baby in there." Then he checked me and said, "There's another baby in here!" Seven minutes later, our son Greg made his appearance. I was in total shock, for sure. I knew, however, that I wanted to be the one to tell Garry. (Dads were not allowed in the delivery room in those days.) At that moment, the doctor told one of the nurses to go get Garry. When Garry arrived at the door, he looked so scared. "Have they told you what we have?" I asked. "No, what do we have?" I said, "We have two boys!" "TWO?" "Yes, two!" "Boys?" "Yes, two boys!" "WOW!" In total shock, he left the room clapping and laughing all the way down the hall. He even called my parents in the middle of the night and told them our news. My mama didn't believe him and told him that preachers weren't supposed to lie!

The reality was that I had no idea how we were going to make it with three babies—two years old and under. *But God* provided! Not too many days later, my mama came bearing lots of gifts. I'm convinced that my kids might not have had anything to wear if it hadn't been for my mama. Plus, our sweet church members helped with our meals and took up a love offering to help us pay the hospital bill. We had no insurance and had only saved up enough money for one baby. We must have thought that we could live off love!

And this same God who takes care of me will supply all your needs from his glorious riches, which have been given to us in Christ Jesus.

Philippians 4:19

11

Chapter 5

I look back now, and mostly, the next years were a complete blur. In 1972 Garry graduated from seminary with a master's in theology. Soon after that, we moved to LaGrange, Georgia. Garry had been asked to be the pastor of Western Heights Baptist Church there. Christen was a little over two years old, and Grant and Greg were six weeks old. Christen was a beautiful, sweet, smart, mature little girl, and she was the perfect big sister. Her brothers were doubly cute and smart, but I have to say that they were double trouble. They kept me super busy.

We built our first little house after living in the parsonage for two years. One night our friends helped us hang our lovely window treatments in our new living room. The next morning, I came down the stairs and saw the boys wiping their grape-jellied hands all over the new curtains. Garry said I looked like Moses coming down off Mt. Sinai, raising and waving my arms while shouting, "WHAT HAVE YOU DONE?" Then there was the time they got into my make-up and rubbed it into our white carpet. I never understood why I chose that white carpet anyway.

The scariest thing they ever did together was when they both climbed up onto the counter-top in the kitchen…one on each side of the stove. One of them turned on the burner, and the other put a cassette tape on it. When I got to them, the tape was smoking, they were giggling and pointing and saying, "Fiah!" (Fire!). I saved us from a house fire that day.

The most embarrassing event happened one week during a revival. Our friend, who was preaching the revival, did magic shows with children. Soon after he arrived at our house, our boys chewed up his magic sponge balls. Then they destroyed one of his cassette tapes by pulling the tape strip out. They were on a roll, indeed.

One afternoon they were napping and the doorbell rang. It was the insurance man collecting his monthly payment. I felt God telling me to invite him to our revival, and we began talking about the Lord. I looked up and the boys were making their way down the stairs. I immediately began to smell something. You guessed it—they had pooped in their pants and had it all over themselves! The insurance guy stammered a bit and asked me, "Is that ch-chocolate?" "No," I answered, "I don't think that's chocolate." Then he must have gotten a whiff of it, and he said, "Well, I'd b-better go!" I don't think he showed up for that revival.

During those days, I was pretty much just surviving as a child of God, wife, and mother. I really struggled. I was so immature, and I didn't know how to be the wife and mother I knew I needed to be. *But God* loved me so much, and He knew I needed help. One day I found myself in a Christian bookstore with Garry. I almost never went into a bookstore. Garry had enough books for the entire world, or so it seemed. But on that day, my eyes caught the title of a book for women, *Today's Woman, Frustrated or Fulfilled?* I bought that book, took it home, read it, and it literally changed my life. It was a scripturally based book that encouraged me in practical ways to love God, love my husband and children, and love and serve others in my life.

And you must love the LORD your God with all your heart, all your soul, all your mind, and all your strength. The second is equally important: Love your neighbor as yourself. No other commandment is greater than these.

Mark 12:30-31

I'm definitely not perfect in any of these relationships, and I've messed up so many times. *But God* is still teaching me, forgiving me, and showing me Grace in all my struggles and failures. No matter what, in those days, I still loved being the mommy of God's greatest blessings to us. I was also so thankful for our sweet babysitters, beautiful friends who loved us, helpful church members, and the fact that we lived close to our families. My mama would visit often. She must have thought I needed help because she would clean my house every time she visited. And it was helpful that the kids adored her and loved playing with her.

We also loved visits from Garry's sister Kathy. Those were my skinny days, and I could just about eat anything without gaining weight. One visit, Kathy and I made tacos. We both ate seven tacos each. That was one of our finest moments!

The kids were in their Aunt Kathy's wedding..

14

*I could still fit into my wedding
dress after three kids.!*

Chapter 6

Be strong in the Lord and in his mighty power. Put on all of God's armor so that you will be able to stand firm against all strategies of the devil.

Ephesians 6:10-11

God blessed our time at Western Heights in an incredible way. We made lifelong friends who loved us despite our youth and inexperience. Garry's passion to see people come to know the Lord was so evident, and the church was growing at an amazing rate. Of course, as we all know, when God is at work and blessing, the enemy is working overtime to see if he can wreak havoc—and he did.

We had been there four years when some little black children came to our Vacation Bible school; they had been given a flyer along with other children at their school. But, oh, the reaction of some church members and members of the community! This was the 1970s, and LaGrange was known to have an active KKK chapter. Rumors spread everywhere! Garry was accused of following the school bus home with the expressed purpose of handing out invitations to the black children so he could integrate the church. The funniest rumor (not funny then) was that I got into a fistfight with someone at church. Both rumors were untrue, of course. I was devastated; I couldn't believe how unkind some people were. There were those who even tried to make it church policy that black people could never enter our church in the future. Garry was ready to resign if that happened.

But God won that battle! Some people left and never came back. During the crisis, a dear friend shared with Garry that he had walked into the local fire and rescue meeting where some guys were saying that should our house happen to catch on fire—with the kids and me inside—they might be a little slow to arrive. The implication was clear. Wow! I'm so thankful for God's love and protection during that time. And, by the way, the good people and good times always outweighed the bad. I still loved being a pastor's wife, and I was still totally in love with the preacher.

Do not be afraid. When you go through deep waters, I will be with you. When you go through rivers of difficulty, you will not drown. When you walk through the fire of oppression, you will not be burned up;
the flames will not consume you.
For I am the LORD, your God.

Isaiah 43:1-3

Chapter 7

Two years passed, God was still blessing, and the church was growing. We were planning on building a new worship center and more educational space. Garry and I were going to build our dream house on a beautiful lake. I was so excited—I was loving the good life that I had always thought we would have. But then something totally unexpected happened to me.

One night in September of 1977, I was awakened in the middle of the night by what sounded like a voice saying strongly to me, *Go unto the uttermost part of the earth.* I looked at Garry, thinking that he had spoken to me—but he was sound asleep. I got out of bed and looked out the window. I didn't know what had just happened, but I told God, "If this is You, then don't let me forget it. But if it's not You, then let me forget." I went back to sleep and didn't wake up until morning; and when I did open my eyes, that phrase, "Go unto the uttermost part of the earth" crossed my mind. Then it hit me: could God be calling me to be a missionary? *But, God???* He wouldn't do that, because I could *never* be a missionary. A couple of years before, I had even told my friend Kay, who was on her way with her husband Mike and five kids to serve as missionaries in Guatemala, that I really admired her, but I could NEVER be a missionary. I was spoiled rotten. I was happy where I was, doing what I thought God wanted me to do. Where would we live? We're about to build our dream house on a lake! Where would our kids be educated? I couldn't leave my family in the United States and go somewhere else. How could I tell Garry? He would think I had lost my mind. So, I just would not tell him. That was my plan. God probably didn't speak to me anyway.

So it began—the most miserable season of my spiritual life. I really knew deep down inside that God was calling me to go, but I refused to respond and obey. I completely shut down my communication with the Lord. I experienced total misery, because as I learned, disobedience leads to an unhappy existence. The words to that old song, "Trust and Obey, for there's no other way to be happy in Jesus, but to Trust and Obey," became very real to me.

17

Jonah had nothing on me—I was totally running from God as far and as fast as I could go. I was so glad I made it through the Lottie Moon Christmas offering time. Lottie Moon had been a Southern Baptist missionary to China. Every December, churches raise money in her honor to support foreign missionaries. All through that December, Garry was preaching some powerful sermons on missions. Why was he doing that? I literally had to hold on tight to the back of the pew so I wouldn't go running down the aisle and make a complete fool of myself.

Then came January. God and I were still at odds, but I finally broke. I told God that I at least would tell Garry about what had happened to me and what I was feeling. It was cold that night, and I was already in bed when Garry got home from a planning meeting at church. He got into bed and pulled the house plans for our dream house out from under the bed and unrolled them. Then I told him, "Garry, before we build that house, I have to tell you something." He rolled the plans up and then looked at me and said, "What is it, Kathy? Has God called you to be a missionary?" Wow! I was in shock. I had never even hinted to him that God was calling me. I asked, "How did you know?" Then he told me his story.

Back in September, he had gone to Columbus, Georgia to make a hospital visit. On his way back, he passed by Callaway Gardens. Our friends Mike and Kay, newly appointed Southern Baptist missionaries, had spent three months in the missionary orientation center there. As he was passing by, he felt strongly that God was calling him to go somewhere outside of the United States to preach and minister. He even pulled over on the side of the road and told God, "I'm willing to go, but You'll have to call Kathy. I can't just go home and tell her that I want to go." When he finished his story, he looked at me and said, "God called you, didn't He? "Yes, He did."

After I told Garry about my experience and my struggle, we cried, prayed, and asked God where He wanted us to go. We even got out an atlas. We decided it should be a Latin American country since I had minored in Spanish in college. That night we were overwhelmed with questions about our future. *But God* let us experience His sweet presence in that room. We had no idea what was next, but we were sure of one thing: He had called us, and we knew He would always be with us. I was still afraid—but fear is a liar.

But ye shall receive power, after that the Holy Ghost is come upon you: and ye shall be witnesses unto me both in Jerusalem, and in all Judea, and in Samaria, and unto the uttermost part of the earth.

Acts 1:8

Flying to Panama, Central America, photo by my dad.

Chapter 8

The next months were totally crazy. We resigned from our church, sold our house, and packed some of our belongings in crates to send to the country of Panama. We were appointed by the Southern Baptist International Mission Board in June of 1978 to go there as missionaries.

Our next adventure was a family trip. Friends let us use their motor home, and we took a long vacation to Washington, DC, Disney World, and Six Flags over Georgia. We made lots of memories before leaving our country. While we were in the D.C. area, we took the kids to a water park in Jamestown, Virginia. Garry and the kids had so much fun going down the huge water slide there. I didn't like to get my hair wet, so water slides were not my favorites. However, they begged me to go down and assured me I could do it without getting my face or hair wet. So, I did it. I started down slowly and was able to control my speed, all the while thinking that this was fun like they said! Then, all of a sudden, this huge young man caught up with me, crashed into my back, and took me at an incredible speed, all the way down. As we splashed into the water, I not only got my hair wet, but I also thought I was going to drown, because he landed on top of me! I finally made it up from the abyss for air and saw the kids and Garry laughing hysterically. I wasn't laughing. And, yes, that was my first and last water slide!

Our trip ended at Six Flags. Our kids have always been adventurous, so they loved all

Appointment Service in Ridgecrest, NC

the rides. As we were winding our way through the Scream Machine line, a gentleman looked at our twins wearing their Alabama shirts and said, "I see you guys live in Alabama. Greg answered him, "No sir, we don't live nowhere." That broke my heart—because we really didn't have a home, and we certainly didn't know what was next.

What came next from September through December was missionary orientation at Callaway Gardens in Pine Mountain, Georgia. We lived in a small cabin in the woods. There we met some beautiful, special people who were going through the same process as we were. During those four months we learned so much about what to expect and how to respond; but until you go, you can never really know.

Our kids had the best time becoming friends with the other missionary kids. They seemed to adjust much better than I did. I'll never forget the sweetest prayer that Christen prayed one night before going to sleep. "Thank you, Jesus, for a place to live and a warm bed to sleep in. And, thank you for my new friends." I needed to be reminded that even the simplest things in life sometimes matter the most.

We had the most special Christmas with our families that year, but goodbyes at the Birmingham Airport later in December were awful. Leaving our family was the hardest thing we had ever done. We flew off into the unknown. I was still afraid, *But God* assured me that we were doing the right thing. We knew He would be with us. On the plane, on our way to language school, Grant looked up at his daddy and asked, "When are we gonna start telling them about Jesus?" That was and still is a profound question. First, we had to learn Spanish, and we arrived in San Jose, Costa Rica, to do just that.

Obey me, and I will be your God, and you will be my people.
Do everything as I say, and all will be well!

Jeremiah 7:23

Chapter 9

Learning a new language as an adult can be tough. It's also extremely difficult living in a foreign country; culture shock strikes when you least expect it. We thought we all were doing pretty well—until about a month after we arrived.

We loved playing board games with our kids, and we had brought *Aggravation* with us. We were playing one night when suddenly the game turned ugly. The kids were angry and were literally knocking each other's playing pieces onto the floor. "There! Take that!" Garry unsuccessfully tried to calm them down. Finally, he said, "Okay, that's it! We are finished. Go to your rooms!" At this point, the kids and I began crying. One of the boys spoke up and said what we were all thinking. "Okay! I don't EVER want to play *Aggravation* in Costa Rica again!" I totally understood.

It was a different life. I mean, we had a tiny little turquoise refrigerator—nothing felt like home. We had no car and no phone, and we felt like children learning how to talk again. Our shower was rigged with an electric contraption called a "widow-maker," which gave us some hot water. Scary. We missed our family, our friends, our church, and our country.

Garry and I celebrated our 10th wedding anniversary in Costa Rica. On the night of our anniversary, we went out to dinner and left the kids home with our maid. (Yes, all the missionaries had a maid, and I'm convinced that we would never have been able to survive without her.) During dinner, we felt a strong earthquake. It shook the room, and the chandelier swayed back and forth. When we got home that night, we found all three of the kids asleep in our bed. We also found a detailed note from Christen telling us what had happened to them. It seemed that while they were playing hide and seek, Grant fell into the toilet and got his foot stuck! Then they experienced their first earthquake. The sweet babies were traumatized and thought they would be safer if they slept together that night. I cried when I saw them snuggled up together.

Our Spanish classes were intense. We weren't allowed to speak English while we were in class. Five days a week for four hours, it was nothing but Spanish for us. Then, besides written homework, we were told to go out in the afternoon and practice what we had learned. At the end of the year, we were actually quite proficient in Spanish, but we did have some very embarrassing moments.

One little guy who Garry tried to talk to on a bus called him *Estupido*. That's an easy word to recognize. On another occasion, Garry asked our neighbor's kids if he could ride their skateboard down the sidewalk. On his way down, he thought he was shouting to them, "Be careful! Move out of the way. I'm falling!" The kids all ran into their house, and their mom came out laughing and talking in broken English. "Do you know what you say? You say, 'Be careful! Move! I am going to the bathroom on myself!'" That was a tough learning experience for Garry, for sure.

One of the scariest things that's ever happened to us happened that year. One afternoon our little family was downtown shopping in a shoe store when I looked up, and I noticed that Grant was missing. He was nowhere in the store! We panicked and looked everywhere outside, but he was not there. Garry and I started running down the sidewalk frantically searching for him. About a block away, we saw him holding a man's hand about to cross the crowded street. To this day, I don't know what I said to that man as we grabbed Grant and ran back. That could have ended differently, *But God* was there to guide us to our little boy.

The most precious thing that could happen in our family also happened in Costa Rica. Christen, Grant, and Greg all asked Jesus to come into their lives there. I can still see them together with Garry, praying. God's Love and Grace are so beautiful!

We truly loved the gorgeous country of Costa Rica. It helped that we made lifelong friends with other missionaries who were just like us and totally understood what we were going through. Plus, my parents came to see us twice, each time bearing gifts for the kids. The last time they came was in December before we left for Panama. We rented a car and took them to some beautiful tourist spots. I was devastated when we left them at the airport.

We were returning the rental car when Garry turned left into a one-way street going the wrong way. He was spotted by the police and got pulled over. The policeman looked very angry as he pulled out his pad to give Garry a ticket. I started crying and blubbering something to him in Spanish. He looked upon me with pity, put the pad and pen back in his pocket, and told Garry, "Tell your Señora that it's going to be alright. You can go." As we pulled away, a confused Garry looked at me and said, "Honey, I don't know exactly what you told him, but you can do that every time I get pulled over if you want to." And, I did—at least one other time when we were back in the U.S. That time I was driving and speeding, and it worked again. Mercy is a good thing.

The faithful love of the LORD never ends! His mercies never cease. Great is his faithfulness; his mercies begin afresh each morning.

Lamentations 3:22-23

My parents' first visit to Costa Rica

Kids' first missionary kids camp

Chapter 10

Garry has always said that we must not have heard God correctly when He called us to the *uttermost* part of the earth, because we ended up in the *bottermost* part of the earth—David, Panama. We arrived in David in January 1980. We were the first IMB missionaries ever to live and work in the province of Chiriqui. It was more than seven hours from the capital, Panama City. We were below sea level, and we went there with no fan or air conditioner and, of course, no telephone. We had one car, which was a stick shift with no air conditioner. We hadn't been there long when Grant told us, "I wish I was lying naked in the snow!" We all laughed, but we wished we were right there with him.

Boquette, Panama

About a month after we arrived, I got really sick. I went to the doctor and found out that I had a raging yeast infection. The doctor told me, "Welcome to Panama." That was not funny to me because I had never been so sick and miserable. I was getting better by Easter Sunday, which became one of the most memorable days of my life.

On that Easter Sunday morning, we had been invited to go up to the mountain town of Boquete for a baptismal service. Garry had been asked to preach that night at the church there. When we arrived in Boquete that morning, we stopped in town for freshly baked bread and a soft drink. And oh, the cool air was so refreshing! We arrived at the beautiful, winding mountain river and I sat down in the grass to wait for the baptism. Suddenly I got the urge to use the bathroom, so I got up to find one—but I soon realized I wouldn't be able to make it to a bathroom in time; as I stood up, I felt something trickling down my legs. I was horrified as I made my way to our van. What was I going to do? No one could ever know about this! I couldn't stay in the car, but at the same time, I couldn't leave my wet clothes on. I was wearing a dress and—oh yes—pantyhose. I began taking everything except my dress off, and I just sat there, thinking: *if I stay here, everybody's going to think I don't want to be here. What should I do?* I decided there was only one thing I could do: I got out of the car and looked for Garry. When I found him, I leaned over and whispered to him, "You're not going to believe this, but I don't have any panties on!" Oh, the shock on his face was priceless! When he composed himself after I told him what had happened, he whispered back into my ear, "If Lottie Moon could just see you now!" It's such a comforting thing to know that I'm probably the only missionary in the history of missionaries who has ever gone to a baptism service with no panties on. That's my story, and I'm sticking to it.

For everything there is a season, a time for every activity under heaven. A time to cry and a time to laugh. A time to grieve and a time to dance.

Ecclesiastes 3:1,4

Chapter 11

So be strong and courageous! Do not be afraid and do not panic
before them. For the LORD your God will personally go ahead of you.
He will neither fail you nor abandon you.

Deuteronomy 31:6

Garry's job in the neighboring provinces of Chiriqui and Bocas Del Toro was to preach, visit pastors of existing churches to encourage them to reach their communities for Christ, and help them start missions. He even pastored the church in David because there was no pastor at the time. However, he wasn't at David every Sunday because he traveled much of the time.

On one of those trips, he left the car at home for me and rode a bus to a mountain town close to the border of Costa Rica. He got out of the bus at the end of the route. From there, he was going to hitch a ride for the next five miles. Meanwhile, he crossed over the border into Costa Rica, bought some snacks, and looked around at the hardware store there. When he crossed back over into Panama, he was stopped, arrested, and taken to the military post. Because he didn't have any identification on him, he was interrogated for six hours and accused of being CIA. Panama was politically unstable at the time, and in that area, a dissident had been found beheaded with his fingers cut off. It was a miracle they didn't take him out and kill him right there; I would've never seen him again. *But God* was with Garry, and he convinced them that he was not CIA and that he was simply making a visit to a church in Monte Lirio. The Lieutenant finally agreed to let him go. The next month Garry visited the military post, thankfully with his head and fingers intact. This time he took the Lieutenant a Bible and all the other officers a calendar. He thanked them for their treatment of him and encouraged them to walk with the Lord.

Living in David was a challenge for our little family. Again, we had no phone or any other method of communication except snail mail. We did break down and buy air conditioners for our bedrooms. We were the only English speakers in our community, and we had no English television or radio. Our only option was to speak in Spanish. I even washed some clothes on the rocks in a nearby river when we had no electricity. Greg broke his arm on a Sunday afternoon when he collided with our dog Darling. Garry took him to the public hospital, and they said, "Yes, it's broken in two places. Bring him back in two weeks, and we'll fix it." That was unacceptable to us, and Garry found a private doctor who set it the next day.

Our kids went to the Spanish-speaking private schools when we first got to David, but after the first year we decided to ask for a Journeyman, a two-year missionary, to teach them. We told our kids that we were getting a Journeyman teacher, and Greg panicked. "Do you mean we're going to have to learn Journeyman? We're already learning Spanish!"

Our church youth met at our house often.

Greg was so happy when we assured him that he was not going to have to learn another language.

Our family loved the beautiful people in our church—especially the youth. We invited them over to our house frequently. I'll never forget our first Christmas there. Our youth thought that all the packages under our tree were fake. How could one family have that many presents? I was embarrassed and needed a reminder that we were so blessed. That Christmas morning, we closed all the windows, turned on the air conditioners in our bedrooms, and let the kids roller-skate all over the house. What a cool, memorable day!

We experienced other very special times in the city of David. On the Panamanian Mother's Day, our youth would sneak into our yard, set off firecrackers, and come to our bedroom window to serenade me with the most

beautiful songs ever! One of the most special times for me as a mom was to watch Garry baptize Christen, Grant, and Greg in a nearby river, along with others who had decided to follow Jesus. For this baptism, I remained fully clothed!

I will forever be grateful for our families and friends who visited us in the "boonies" while living there. My parents, my sister Ann Marie and her family, Garry's parents, and his sister Kathy, all made their way to the tropics to see us. We took them to all the cooler places and loved every minute. Of course, taking them all to the Panama Canal was always on our agenda. There's no place quite like it. On each visit, my daddy, a WWII Army veteran and retired colonel with the National Guard would always go to the commissary to buy us special things that we couldn't find in our grocery stores. He always bought me Dr Peppers, and they were like gold to me. It's crazy that when you're not able to get something, you want it even more than before. One lesson I learned while we were there was how very blessed we North Americans are. No doubt about it.

So many good things happened while we lived in David, but I also experienced the darkest personal struggle of my life. I began to think that my daddy didn't love me and that he never had. Satan brought up so many memories that I thought validated that feeling. My daddy was a great provider for our family, but I needed more from him. I needed to be affirmed, hugged, and told I was loved. He never really knew how to do that. I spent many years struggling with the perception that he didn't love me, and I'm sad to say that I stayed in the pit of unforgiveness and insecurity for a long time. *But God*, in time, healed my heart, and I

Baptism at the River

realized that my daddy did love me—very much. He just had a different way of showing it. He had parented the way he was parented. I'll always be so grateful for that time of struggle because it made me realize how much my Heavenly Father loves and values me. And I'm still remembering how much my earthly daddy loved me. He showed me love by his generous giving to me throughout my lifetime. He financially blessed my family and me more than we could have ever imagined.

*See how very much our Father loves us,
for he calls us his children, and that is what we are!*

1 John 3:1a

The youth group, Garry, and our kids at the beach

Garry's parents and sister Kathy visited.

My parents with their grandchildren

Garry in his office with
his hundreds of books

Christen ready to
go to school

31

Chapter 12

Because of our ministry with the young people in David, the Panama Baptist Convention requested that we move to Panama City for our second term of service and work with the students at the University of Panama. When we went back from our first furlough in the States, our house was being renovated. It was an old wooden typical tropical house on stilts, and it was located right on

Our house in Panama City

the edge of Ancon Hill. The U.S. Armed Forces Southern Command was also located on and inside that hill. If you climbed Ancon you could look down onto the Panama Canal. The house was directly across the highway from Panama City. Monkeys played in our mango tree in the front yard, and iguanas and sloths visited our backyard frequently.

Every day Garry would go to the university past Panamanian soldiers carrying M-16's. It was a well-known fact that communists were on campus spreading their propaganda, making it so important for Garry to share the Gospel. Many students' lives were changed during those years. They became followers of Jesus and were discipled and trained to tell others about Him. Then they began planting churches. Twelve churches were started by Garry and that group of young university students who called themselves *Los Brigadistas*— The Brigades.

We loved having the university students in our home. Sometimes we would cook out, and other times they would cook for us. They were amazing cooks, and they

The Brigades

would just come in and take over my kitchen. Our times of worship and fun will always hold a special place in my heart. They became like family to us. They fondly

32

called Garry "Papa." Oh, the memories our family made with those students!

I realized in those days why God had wanted us to go to Panama; He allowed us to invest our lives in the future generation of Christians in that beautiful country. I was so thankful that God had asked us to join Him there.

Even now, those wonderful students are the pastors, wives, and professional leaders of Panama. Today, so many years later, they are still making a difference in the lives of many other Panamanians. I didn't realize it then, *But God* indeed had a plan when He called us there, and I'm so grateful I didn't miss it.

> *What shall we say about such wonderful things as these? If God is for us, who can ever be against us?*
>
> Romans 8:31

Photos of University students at our house, Panama City, Panama

Photos of University Students at our house Panama City, Panama

Chapter 13

Even though God was working, we experienced some pretty scary times in Panama. Garry got Dengue Fever and lost twenty pounds in two weeks. Once he came home from a trip and his fever was so high he was delirious. I had to call a doctor friend from the Canal zone to come to our house and treat him. One night, Garry woke me up and told me he was a little uncomfortable and was going to take a walk. I went back to sleep and was awakened by a phone call from a nurse at Gorgas Hospital, a U.S. government hospital, about three blocks from our house. Garry had a kidney stone and had walked himself there and asked for help. The following days were painful even to think about.

Then, there was the night Garry boarded a banana boat in the Bay of Panama and headed for the Darien Jungle. A strong storm blew up and raged all night. For hours, the boat—with its passengers and crew—was in danger of capsizing. People were crying, screaming, and begging God to save them. Even Garry thought they weren't going to make it. *But God* calmed that storm. Garry lost the supper I had packed for him, but at least he didn't lose his life.

Fire set by protesters at the docks on the Panama Canal, photo by Garry

The entire time we were in Panama, the country was in a state of political unrest. On one of those days, Garry again found himself in the wrong place at the wrong time. He was parked in front of Balboa High School and was standing next to his car, waiting for me to come out, when he heard shots fired. He looked back, and protesters were running from the canal docks toward him. They were running away from the Panamanian Army who was shooting at them, toward Garry. Once they got close to him, Garry started running as fast as he could, too. As I watched from a window, it appeared that he was leading the crowd away from the army. He raced to the side of the school and ran inside, safe once again.

My favorite God story in Panama happened one Sunday evening. Garry was invited to preach in the Cuna Indigenous Church in downtown Panama. The kids and I let him off near the church and headed back to our church in Balboa. He had been walking for a couple of blocks when a little girl approached him and said, "Señor, they are going to rob you!" He looked back and saw two guys coming up behind him. He just kept walking. As they came closer, Garry stopped,

34

turned around, and punched one of them in the throat. They ran off when an old man in an apartment building started yelling, "Robbers! Robbers!" Garry continued walking and finally made it to the church. A few minutes later, the little girl entered the church and found him. She said, "Señor, they are waiting for you at the corner." He thanked her and explained to her that he would be staying there awhile. He told her that she was welcome to stay, too. He turned around to speak to the pastor, and when he looked back, she was gone. Was she an angel? Maybe. *But God* used her that day to protect Garry from harm. Oh, and I was so glad that my main man, a Special Forces wannabe, still knew how to fight.

God is our refuge and strength, always ready to help in times of trouble.

Psalms 46:1

Garry traveled to many islands, via boats large and small.

35

Chapter 14

Panama is a beautiful country full of culture and history, and we all reaped its benefits. Not only was God with us every step we took, but He also allowed us to experience such good times as a family.

All the fear I had about where our kids would be educated was totally unfounded. Besides their experiences with homeschooling, Spanish-speaking Catholic schools, and the Journeyman in David, they also attended an English-speaking Catholic school and Department of Defense schools in Panama City. It was more than an education; it was a life experience that resulted in an excellent education. They were all inducted into the National Honor Society in the DOD schools.

Christen was a cheerleader at Balboa High School; she also paddled a kayak with a team of girls and other teams of young men and women through the Panama Canal. Grant and Greg were on the swimming and diving teams at Curundu Junior High; they were also self-taught gymnasts and had the opportunity to practice with the Panama National Gymnastics team. Garry and I, along with my parents, even got to board a tugboat on the Canal and help the Pilot push a ship through the locks. What incredible and unforgettable experiences!

It was such a blessing for us to love on and work with the beautiful people of Panama. While we were in Panama City, Garry got to be the pastor of La Iglesia Bautista La Boca, and I taught English to the students in our seminary. Plus, we were able to work alongside some of the most amazing God-sent missionaries. They, too, were our family.

As always, time passed quickly, and our time in Panama had to come to an end. In 1988, Christen graduated from Balboa High School, we said goodbye to our friends in beautiful Panama, and we headed to the states for a furlough .

Chapter 15

Furloughs were always a huge blessing for our family. Shades Mountain Baptist Church in Birmingham always provided housing for us. Dr. Charles T. Carter was a wonderful pastor. He was, from the beginning, a great support to us and our work. We love him and Janice very much!

We got to travel, preach, and speak in many churches that were very supportive of our ministry. Our kids told Garry on numerous occasions that they could preach his sermon, as he preached the same one in all the places we visited. He even occasionally used a couple of Spanish words in his sermons; because he had been accustomed to preaching in Spanish, he sometimes couldn't think of the word in English. The kids and I were amused, and we let him know!

I can't even explain how wonderful it was being back home with our families. Garry's mama cooked the most delicious fresh peas, fresh corn, and cornbread I had ever tasted. There was none like it anywhere. My mama was also an amazing cook. Her dumplings were to die for! She always cooked the best dishes and desserts to go with the steaks my daddy cooked out on the grill. We were totally spoiled with the best meat anywhere because my daddy was the founder, owner, and CEO of his own meatpacking company. How could we not love being there?

We loved being with family, but we couldn't help noticing that sometimes it was hard on our kids as they adjusted—once again—to a new place, new people, and new schools. I have to admit that it was also hard for me to adjust to life in the States again. Going to the grocery store was frustrating; there were too many items to choose from. Why did the United States need this much stuff? It just seemed so unnecessary.

Plus, at first, I disliked going shopping for clothes for myself. I knew I had to buy new clothes because my sister Ann Marie had warned me, "You had better not come back to the States looking like a frumpy missionary!" Well, alrighty, then! But I didn't know where to start—big department stores overwhelmed me. I did, however, manage to buy some "non-frumpy" clothes. I think my sister was pleased.

By the time I got used to shopping and grocery stores again, it was time to go back. I may have even stuffed our suitcases with some of those *unnecessary* U.S. items to take back with me. Those things made me feel a little better because goodbyes were always awful.

Chapter 16

The furlough after we left Panama was way too short. Garry was asked by the IMB to be the Associate Area Director for Middle America and Canada. His job was to help manage the work and support over 300 missionaries in seven countries. The area office was in Guatemala. So, after a few short months in the states, Garry, the boys, and I headed to our new home there.

It was definitely the most challenging move I had ever made because we had to leave Christen in Birmingham at Samford University. I cried all during her senior year. I'm sure I was just preparing myself for the worst separation I had ever known up to that point. What made it even more difficult is that we didn't have a phone. We figured out a way to talk to her, though; every Sunday at 2:00, we all walked a block to a construction site and received a call from her and my parents. It wasn't a pretty place; it was a dirty little shack where we occasionally saw mice running around. But it was my favorite part of the week. My biggest daily struggle about being in a foreign country was definitely being so far away from her. I learned more about trusting God in those days than I ever had before. I knew He loved her more than I ever could, and I knew how very much I loved her. It was more important than ever for me to remember that God had called me to be a missionary, too. I realized that all this fit into His plan for all of our lives. Not having Christen with us was just so very hard for me.

She did get to visit us, though. Her longest visit was during the Jan-term of her freshman year. While she was with us, we were a family again, and it just seemed so right. She had even brought presents and clothes to the kids who lived at the site where we received her calls. She loved them, and they loved her right back.

When it was time for her to go back to Samford, it was the saddest day for all of us. The boys, Garry, and I couldn't even talk on the way back from the airport. After we left her, we took Grant and Greg to school, and then Garry and I went home.

Christen's first visit to Guatemala, Central America

I ran to the kitchen because I remembered that she had wanted to take some pineapple back with her. I found the pineapple still in the refrigerator, and I lost it; I ran upstairs yelling, "She forgot her pineapple!" I passed her room, and it smelled so sweet, just like her. I found Garry in our room crying. Then we hugged, hung onto each other, and shook and cried. I didn't know if we would ever get over not being closer to her.

It became a little easier for us when Christen met Rob, her future husband, at Samford. The thing is that she probably wouldn't have even gone to Samford if we had stayed in the States and never become missionaries to Panama and Guatemala.

Photos taken at La Aurora Airport in Guatemala City

But God just kept showing us that the plan He had for us was so much better than anything we could have ever planned for ourselves. God is Good like that!

"For I know the plans I have for you," says the LORD. "They are plans for good and not for disaster, to give you a future and a hope."
Jeremiah 29:11

Chapter 17

Being in Guatemala for Garry, the boys, and me was so different than being in Panama. Garry often traveled all over Central America visiting missionaries. Some of his responsibilities also took him regularly to Richmond, Virginia, Hollywood, Florida, and El Paso, Texas. I was just so thankful for the times he got to be home with us.

After we arrived in Guatemala, while waiting for our house to be finished, we lived in a rental house. The first time I washed clothes and went outside to hang them on the clothesline, I heard a huge *BANG*. I looked around and the wind had blown the steel door shut, and I was

Volcán Agua in Antigua, Guatemala, photo by Grant

locked out. So, picture this: I was surrounded by eight-foot cement block walls with razor wire on top. I panicked until I saw a built-in brick fire pit. I managed to climb on top of the fire pit and step up onto the wall—I was pretty impressed with myself because I was petrified of heights. We shared a wall with our neighbors, so I began to call out, weakly, "Hola! Hola! Hola!" Miraculously, my neighbor heard me and came out to see this crazy gringa standing on her eight-foot wall. She got a ladder and helped me down. She let me use her phone to locate Garry, and he came to the rescue. I sure was grateful he was in the country that day.

Grant and Greg started a new school when we arrived in Guatemala—the Christian Academy of Guatemala. They were able to make friends with missionary kids whose parents were located in the city. It was an excellent experience; their classes were small, and they had amazing teachers. They played soccer, basketball, and volleyball on their school team and competed with other local schools.

Along with their dad and some friends from school, the boys climbed Volcano Agua during their senior year. The group accidentally went off the path and got lost. They spent three hours in the dark climbing up the side of the mountain. I'm glad I didn't know what had happened until they got back! Grant and Greg even learned to drive in Guatemala, which was, and still is, a very scary thought.

I was so thankful for them during those days. They were both there for me when Garry was traveling. One day I had gone downtown to exchange dollars for quetzals, the Guatemalan currency. I was waiting in the front office of the money exchange business when suddenly a group of armed men burst into the office, waving their guns and shouting. I got up and ran into an inner office. I was so scared, *But God* gave me the presence of mind to remove my wedding rings and other jewelry and put them into my skirt pocket. Minutes later, a couple of them came in and pointed their guns right toward my chest and said, "Give us everything you have!" I gave them everything that was in my purse. Then they told me not to leave for 20 minutes, or they would kill me. That day they got my checkbook, my watch, and some money I had in my wallet. They also took my peace of mind for a long time, because I was completely traumatized. Garry was in Mexico during those days, so our boys became my protectors. Everywhere we went, they flanked me. That's what I choose to remember about those awful days. Two bodyguards are much better than one—anytime, anywhere.

Garry was not gone all the time, so we were able to do missionary work in Guatemala in between his trips. Our family, along with some members of the community, started a church. The building we met in was a house that we turned into a church; we named it Antioquia—Antioch. Garry preached and pastored, Greg was the worship leader, Grant played the Casio piano, and I taught the youth in Sunday school. Many people came to know Jesus, and Garry baptized them in a small kid's plastic pool in the backyard. Those were some sweet times for us, and I'm so thankful that Antioquia is still alive today. Again, God let us be a part of His beautiful, amazing plan.

Therefore, go and make disciples of all the nations, baptizing them in the name of the Father and the Son and the Holy Spirit. Teach these new disciples to obey all the commands I have given you. And be sure of this: I am with you always, even to the end of the age.

Matthew 28:19-20

Chapter 18

For me, the boys' high school days ended way too soon. In 1991, they graduated from high school in the beautiful city of Antigua as valedictorian and salutatorian. We then left Guatemala for a long furlough. That fall, they started studying Pre-Med at Auburn University, and Christen began her senior year at Samford. I taught Spanish that year, and Garry attended school once again and earned another master's degree—this time in counseling.

Christen and Rob were married after their graduation from Samford in June of 1992. I thought I was going to have to pick Garry up off the floor the night of the wedding—emotions ran high for all of us. He walked our beautiful Christen down the aisle, gave her away, and then turned around and performed the ceremony. It was almost too much as I watched them, with tears in their eyes, say goodbye to each other as Christen and Rob left after the reception.

The goodbyes, later that summer, were too hard for me to even think about. We left all our kids in the States, and Garry and I returned to Guatemala. It's difficult to explain how extremely sad I was without my

kids. In fact, Garry had to use some of his counseling knowledge on me. I felt lost and alone with no purpose. Garry traveled all the time, so during those days, I was alone in our gated community. It really wasn't safe for me to leave by myself. I was seriously depressed.

But God let me know He was with me and that He wasn't finished with me yet. He allowed me to start a Bible study with the women in our little condo community. It turned out to be one of my greatest blessings as a missionary; I got to know and love my neighbors in a special way, and I got to share my faith and my love for Jesus with them. Plus, I realized once again how much I loved working with women and encouraging them to love God and others more. God truly does fill the emptiness that difficult life situations present when we're least expecting it. I just love it when He does that!

I absolutely loved Guatemala, its people, and the other missionaries we worked with while we were there. When we weren't working, we were playing *Garbage* (cards), watching an occasional college football game together, eating amazing food, and enjoying the beautiful country and its culture. I truly thought we would be there until we retired. But again, God had other plans for us.

Chapter 19

In 1995, our lives changed drastically. We were in the States for Grant and Greg's graduation from Auburn. They were preparing to enter med school at the University of Alabama in Birmingham. While we were there, our first grandchild Kayla was born. It's so very special when the children you love have children you love. There's nothing in the world quite like it!

I got to spend two weeks with that precious little blessing and her parents Christen and Rob, and then I had to leave again. Those dreaded goodbyes were awful. When I got into my car in Chattanooga, Tennessee and headed to Birmingham for my flight back to Guatemala, I couldn't even see to drive. I was a wet mess—I sobbed all the way to Birmingham. I had no idea when I would see them again, and my heart was breaking.

That goodbye was in March, and in the fall of that year we got a call from the senior pastor of First Baptist Church, Jonesboro, Georgia, Dr. Charles Q. Carter. Dr. Carter, a great friend and mentor, asked Garry if he would consider returning to the States to work as his executive pastor.

At first, Garry's response was, "No"; but after much prayer, in the spring of 1996, we left Guatemala and moved to Georgia once again.

It really was an unexpected move for us, because we thought we would be international missionaries for life. *But God* gave us an overwhelming peace that we were doing the right thing, and we left the international mission field after 18 years. After all, in the past year, Garry had logged over 100,000 miles on one major airline alone—not counting the mileage he had accumulated on the small airlines he flew to the countries in Central America. He had become a frequent flyer, and our ministry together was suffering. I seriously couldn't wait to see what God was about to do with us in the coming years.

And let the peace that comes from Christ rule in your hearts...

Colossians 3:15

Chapter 20

I will always believe that God knew just what I needed when He took us to Jonesboro. For me, it was a period of reprieve and allowing God to minister to me. I didn't realize how tired I was, emotionally and physically. No one there had any expectations where I was concerned. It was refreshing.

Also, I never could have imagined how wonderful it was, being a grandmother to little Kayla. She named us *Tito* and *Tita*. We were thinking we would like to be called *Mamita* and *Papito*, but what Kayla started calling me was "Tee Tee." I told Garry that I could be "Tee Tee" and he could be "Pee Pee," but he was not so fond of that idea. So, *Tito* and *Tita* it was. Those names were, and still are, music to our ears!

When Kayla was 18 months old, her sister—our precious Morgan—was born. Then eighteen months later, on his sister Kayla's third birthday, our first grandson Andrew came into our world. It was an incredible experience to be present in the room for his birth. I could never have believed what joy and blessings were to follow! *But God*, who is the giver of wonderful gifts, knew.

While we were in Jonesboro, Garry learned how to get to every hospital in Atlanta and visit the sick. He also preached at times and managed the staff. We loved Charles Q., his wife Margaret, the beautiful people, and the wonderful worship experiences there. I worked with preschoolers in Sunday school, did some substitute teaching in Spanish, and along with my new friend Nancy, started an interior design business. I've always loved decorating, but I really loved making clients happy by making their homes beautiful. And Garry loved that I was spending other people's money instead of his to satisfy my desire to decorate.

Nancy and I had a great time, but we became forever-friends and family when we introduced our children Grant and Shelley to each other. Before we left Jonesboro, they were married. Some months after that, Greg and Lee Anne were married also. They had met as children at Shades Mountain Baptist Church when we were on our first furlough. They were just kids, but when we left to go back to Panama, she wrote on the rafters of her attic, "I might love Greg."

Sometimes I think about how different our lives would have been if I had continued to say "No" to God's plan for my life. I know one thing—our kids would have never met their spouses if we had not gone where God wanted us. It scares me to think that choosing not to obey God could have changed my life and those I love. Obedience, no matter how hard it is, wins. Every. Time.

Greg and Grant's Med School Graduation

Med School Graduation Party

Greg and Lee Anne

Grant and Shelley

*Perry Family:
Rob, Christen, Kayla,
Morgan, and Andrew*

And this is love: that we walk in obedience to his commands. As you have heard from the beginning, his command is that you walk in love.

2 John 1:6 (NIV)

Be careful to obey all these commands I am giving you.
Show love to the LORD your God by walking in his ways
and holding tightly to him.

Deuteronomy 11:22

Chapter 21

If there's one thing I've learned in my lifetime, it's that not everything that happens to us is good. Life is hard. We all struggle. We all disappoint others. We all hurt each other. We all sin. All families experience heartbreak.

My brother Jim lived a tormented life addicted to alcohol and gambling. He knew Jesus, but he didn't live like he did. He wanted to do the right thing, but he always struggled. One night he even went to my parents' house with a loaded gun and told them he was going to shoot them and then kill himself. They were terrified and ran and hid from him. He finally left. My parents lived with the pain and hurt of Jim's addiction almost constantly. They bailed him out of jail and even paid off his gambling debts because his life was in danger.

While we were at Jonesboro, Jim called my parents and told them he was sorry for all the hurt and disappointment he had caused them. Of course, they forgave him because they loved him. About six months after that, Jim was in a horrible tractor accident. It didn't seem life-threatening, but he did flat-line when they got him to the hospital. They revived him but were watching him carefully. I got to visit him the week after his accident. The last thing he said to me was, "I love you, Kat." "I love you, too, Jim," I answered.

I will never forget the shock and despair I felt when we got the call that Jim had died. I couldn't believe it—he was only 51 years old. I will always believe that God let him live after the accident so he could repent and express a desire for a changed life. And in fact, that's exactly what he did. He had shared with his wife Anne, that when he got out of the hospital, he was never going to take another drink and that they were going to start going to church. Even though we were devastated, we knew that one day we would see him again.

There are some other things I've learned in my lifetime: repentance is beautiful; forgiveness is divine. We experience terrible loss, *But God* is close to the brokenhearted and saves those who are crushed in Spirit.

The LORD is close to the brokenhearted;
he rescues those whose spirits are crushed.

Psalms 34:18

Mom and Dad's 50th Anniversary with grandkids (Top Left) Dina, Stephanie, Mark, Christen, Laurie, (Bottom) Grant, Dad, Mom, Greg

Mom and Dad's 50th Anniversary with kids (L-R): Doug and Ann Marie Parsons, Jim and Anne Scogin, Garry and Kathy Eudy, Dad and Mom

Chapter 22

I was sure that Jonesboro wasn't our final step with God because I knew that Garry wanted to pastor a church again. That's when Central Baptist Church in Douglasville, Georgia, found us and asked Garry to be their pastor. It was as if God was finally, after taking us on a beautiful detour, allowing us to live out our first calling as pastor and pastor's wife.

It's hard to describe the love I had for the beautiful people of Central. I learned so much from some very special friends. Bonnie inspired me to forgive, even when the person who hurts you doesn't ask for forgiveness. Brenda was a beautiful servant of Jesus and encouraged me. They both helped me start a women's ministry, which included large special events and a weekly Bible study. Those days with all the women involved in the Bible study will live in my heart as some of the sweetest times in my ministry. We were real with each other, and we all struggled with different issues—*But God* is greater than all our struggles and regrets. He is an Amazing and Compassionate God, and He helped us to love and encourage each other.

Central Baptist Church

We had some of our best times when we were able to get away and attend special events. On one of those trips, I was driving Bonnie's SUV, and my foot got a little heavy. And, wouldn't you know? I got pulled over. When the police officer walked up to the car, Brenda stuck her head out of the window and said, in her sweet south Georgia accent, "Oh, pleasssse, Mr. Officer, don't give her a ticket! She's our pastor's wife, and we're on our way to a Christian women's conference in Pigeon Forge." Thanks to Brenda, he showed mercy and just told me to slow down. Who could not have responded favorably to that precious plea from my friend? Every pastor's wife needs loving friends like I had, who knew everything about me but loved and supported me anyway. I call them my forever friends.

A friend is always loyal, and a brother is born to help in time of need.
Proverbs 17:17

Bonnie, Brenda, Vickie, and Kathy

Gloria, Brenda, Bonnie, Kathy, Lesa, Stephanie, and Melinda

Joyce, Bonnie, Kathy, Brenda, Vickie

Chapter 23

While we were at Central, God blessed us in an incredible way. The church grew rapidly. God let us see the building of a new worship center, a family life center—and finally—our dream house. My forever friend Joyce helped me make it into a beautiful home.

My most embarrassing moment EVER happened on the day we were moving into our new home. A group of deacons was about to help move our furniture in. I decided I needed a bathroom break, so I made my way to the master bathroom and sat down. After a moment, I heard voices in the hall coming toward my room, but really didn't worry until suddenly the potty room door was opened—and there I sat! One of the shocked deacons breathed out loudly, "OH LORD!" and quickly shut the door. And there I still sat. I could hear them scurrying back down the hallway—probably in more shock than I was. We got over it, though. Or, did we? Maybe. I'm still not totally sure.

Garry breaking ground for Central's family life Center

Garry and I at Central's Round Up Outreach Ministry

Not long after we moved in, my parents moved in with us. Several years before, my daddy had to undergo multiple bypass surgery—he had been misdiagnosed with asthma and was being treated for that instead of heart problems. During the emergency surgery, his heart stopped beating for quite some time. Later, my very private daddy told my mama that he had gone up through a tunnel toward a bright light. Then he heard this, "...*I am the resurrection and the life. Anyone who believes in me will live... even after dying.*" John 11:25.

I will always believe that my daddy died that day and was brought back to life. Even the nurses who'd observed him in surgery asked him to share what happened to him, but he only shared it with my mama. However, right after surgery, He told Garry that Jesus said to him, "*I am the resurrection and the life.*" For some reason, he wanted Garry to know. He really had come to love and respect Garry very much.

In the years after his surgery, my daddy never fully recovered. We knew when they moved in with us that he probably didn't have much time left on this earth. He did, however, get to experience some good times with us—and one especially beautiful day with our family.

Our son Greg and his wife Lee Anne were told before they were married that they would never be able to have children because Lee Anne was in a state of premature ovarian failure. We were saddened by this news, but we all knew that God was in control of everything and would make a way for them to grow their family, probably through adoption.

However, one weekend when the kids were visiting, I became suspicious that Lee Anne might be expecting. She was really sick and couldn't stand the smell of the delicious fried chicken and shrimp dinner my mama was preparing. Being the nosy mother-in-law that I was, I just asked her—"You couldn't be pregnant, could you?" Her answer was a definitive "No." I then felt bad for bringing it up. As we were gathering for dinner, Greg asked to say the blessing. He said a beautiful prayer, and then before finishing said, "And God, thank You so much that Lee Anne is pregnant!" WOW! WHAT?! We all began shouting and laughing and asking, "How? When?" They had not planned to tell us about the pregnancy yet, but they thought I was onto them so decided to tell us their miraculous story: They were on a mission trip to Guatemala when the leader of their team, a Guatemalan doctor, asked Lee Anne if they had children. When he learned they weren't able to conceive, he asked if he and the team could pray for them. That night, as the team gathered around Greg and Lee Anne, the doctor prayed a very passionate prayer. No one else knew the reason for the prayer, but Greg and Lee Anne felt God's powerful presence in the room. There was another Guatemalan doctor there

that night, and he told them that during his prayer, he felt that God let him know they were going to have children. At the time, they really didn't know what to think.

Six weeks later, Lee Anne went to the doctor and found out she was pregnant. She wanted to know how far along she was, so she asked. You have to know the answer—six weeks! Six weeks to the day of that prayer in Guatemala! For us, it was an incredible miracle. My daddy didn't live to see Samuel born—Daddy died in early June, and Samuel was born on June 18th—but at least he got to hear the miraculous story of his conception. He also got to hear

that Grant and Shelley were expecting Michael, who was born July 25th, five weeks after Samuel. *But God* was not finished giving us our other greatest blessings until after Daniel (brother to Samuel), Jared (brother to Michael), and Kaylee (sister to Michael and Jared) all came into this world. So, then there were eight. We are unbelievably blessed and so very thankful for each of their precious lives.

All three of our kids with their families

Chapter 24

If anyone tells you that caregiving is easy, don't believe them. Even though I loved my mama so very much, it was still hard. After my daddy's death, it seemed as though she changed and lost her identity. He had been her life.

It was hard for me because I felt responsible for her now. Yet, it seemed as though she wanted to control me and tell me what to do. For a while, she would get mad at me every time I left the house to do something by myself or with a friend. On one of those occasions, I spent the afternoon with my forever friend Vickie who loved and supported me with her prayers and advice. Mama told Garry that I had stayed with Vickie for six hours, and she didn't like it! Garry was supportive of me, but he was also diplomatic and loving to my mama. There were other occasions when Garry had to be the referee and tell us both to behave. He never took my side in her presence, because I had told him not to. Garry became Mama's favorite, and she loved him like a son. He loved her, too—most nights before she went to bed, he rubbed her feet with a soothing lotion. Who wouldn't love that?

During those days, we also had some good moments. We had fun times shopping together. We always liked to try on clothes and let each other approve or disapprove. On one occasion, Mama called out to me from her dressing room, "I'm coming out—I want you to see this skirt!" I opened my door, and the skirt looked nice, but there she stood with NOTHING on from the waist up! I was horrified, but she calmly said, "I can't stand wearing a bra anymore!" Well, alrighty then!

Taking her to doctor visits was always entertaining, too. Once, as we were walking into the doctor's office, she said to me, "I hope this doctor is good-looking. I'm tired of old doctors." Well, what do you know? In walked Dr. McDreamy, a good-looking California surfer type. She was very happy to see him and told him how much she loved young doctors. According to her, they were much easier on the eyes and were smarter than the old ones. She let me know that she was neither blind nor dead yet!

Another time, I took her to a new eye doctor, and she couldn't see him very well because her eyes had been dilated. She asked him, "What do you look like? I can't see you." His nurse answered, "He looks like Brad Pitt." Mama replied, "Wow! I'm missing a blessing!" Yes. The blessing was all mine on that day.

Chapter 25

After twelve amazing years as pastor of Central, Garry felt God leading him to retire from pastoring. It was so very hard for me to leave our church, because that was where I felt fulfilled in my ministry with women. *But God* said to do it, so we did it—not really knowing what was next. And going with my cowboy boot-wearing preacher made it a little easier.

The beautiful people of Central gave us a special good-bye celebration and gifted us with an amazing retirement cruise leaving from New York City going into Canada and back. It was simply incredible and unforgettable.

We sold our dream house and built another one—this time in the mountains of East Tennessee. I couldn't believe we'd be living on Rocking Chair Lane. I just knew we were going to love it when our first Christmas there was the most beautiful white Christmas I could've ever imagined. It was truly magnificent. And God did a special thing every morning and night as He gave us an awesome view of the mountains from every room in the house.

For a while, we had a nice routine. Garry got up every morning, prepared breakfast for Mama, and brought me coffee in bed. Then I would have my second cup on the back deck, looking at God's amazing creation and taking tons of pictures. Living in the Pigeon Forge, Gatlinburg, Townsend area was such fun! Mama, Garry, and I enjoyed everything about it, including the precious people of

62

Valley View Baptist Church in Wears Valley. They reached out to us and became great friends. At times it felt like we were on a permanent vacation. I quickly became an official mountain woman; I even killed a snake all by myself! The bears that visited were so special. Who could ask for more?

The whole retirement thing didn't last very long, though. We might have been enjoying the rocking chair concept, *But God* wasn't finished with us yet. Garry wanted to begin taking pastors and other volunteers from the states to Guatemala to partner with pastors there to support them and help them reach their communities for Christ. He wanted to take construction teams, medical teams, sports teams, evangelistic teams, and teams to work with children in schools. So, the first year of our retirement, Garry formed a non-profit organization and named it E3 Volunteers in order to Equip, Engage, and Empower those who would go with him. That year he took four teams to Guatemala.

Before Garry left on one of those trips, he told me that he wanted to teach me how to shoot a gun. Obviously, he thought I would feel safe if I learned. I will never forget when he took me to the back deck, showed me how to hold the gun properly, and told me to pull the trigger. I'm sure my scream echoed for miles as I fell back, thinking something had kicked me. Well, my shooting days didn't last long; there's a first time and a last time for everything, I guess.

Garry, thinking I was hopeless and helpless, then took me to the front door to say goodbye. He wrapped his arms around me and began praying for me. "God, please take care of Kathy while I'm gone because she needs Your help. And please give her sense enough to call someone to come take care of her mom so that she can get out of the house. You know she needs that, Lord. Amen." And I said an "AMEN!" to that prayer, too. I knew he was right.

Kayla behind Jared, holding Kaylee with Morgan, Andrew, Samuel, Michael, and Daniel

Chapter 26

When Garry was at home we enjoyed God's beautiful Smoky Mountains. He would drive me around in his MR2 Spyder sports car on all the mountain roads. He loved doing the Tail of the Dragon road and could almost keep up with the motorcycles racing around the 11 miles of 318 curves.

One beautiful day he drove me to the mall in Knoxville. After picking me up from shopping, he parked the car for a moment while I put my packages behind the seat. The next thing we knew, an 18-wheeler was backing up toward us, and he smashed our sports car's front end like a bug! I looked up just as he was hitting us, and I actually thought we were dead. Garry and I both got out. Garry, as always, was very nice to the driver, but all I could think to say was, "You're in BIG trouble!" We found some awesome east Tennessee boys to fix it, though, and all was good.

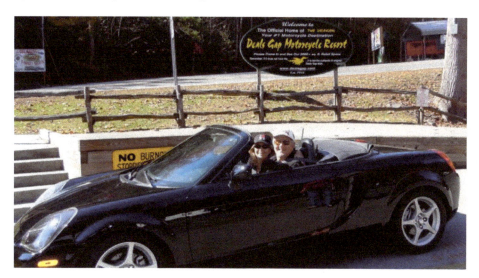

Sometimes it seemed that drama followed us everywhere. On one Sunday afternoon, Garry and I arrived home from church to find that we couldn't drive our SUV down the driveway into the carport because some young guys had come to cut down a dead tree on our property. Garry had previously told them not to come on Sunday because he didn't want them working on Sunday. But there they were anyway, blocking us from getting to our house.

Once we were able to get to the house, we had not been there ten minutes when I looked out our window and realized that our car was on fire! Even though Garry and the boys tried to put it out, the car burned out of control and was a total loss. We realized that if we had been able to park the car in the carport, our house would've caught fire, too. Because the volunteer fire department was miles away, we could have possibly lost everything—even our lives. *But God* was our Protector that day. He's a good, good Father! In all our drama, He's always there!

I look up to the mountains – does my help come from there? My help comes from the LORD, who made heaven and earth!

Psalms 121:1-2

Chapter 27

As time passed, I began to notice that Garry might have the *Universal Man's Disease*—hearing loss. The first time I realized he couldn't hear well was when we were at a store in Pigeon Forge buying supplies for our home. Garry put the toilet paper and paper towels on the conveyor belt, and the

girl at the register asked him, "How many do you have?" Garry answered, "Oh, we're fine! How are you?"

Then there was the time when I had a broken foot and we traveled to Samford University in Birmingham for Kayla's piano recital. Christen met us at the door and asked, "How's your foot?" Garry said, "Oh, it was fine, but it rained on us a little."

Once I told him I needed a new rug. He responded, "Why do you need a new drug?" Another time I offered him chips made with spinach and kale. He asked, "Why would you say that it is spinach from hell?"

We were on our cruise to Canada, and the cruise director asked us if we had enjoyed our trip to Halifax. Garry looked troubled and asked me, "Why would she ask us if we liked our trip to hell and back?"

On another occasion, Garry had just gotten home from Guatemala, and his assistant called him and asked him, "Did you get rested?" Garry's response was, "Why would I get arrested?"

Even though he got hearing aids, the craziness continued. I sometimes wondered if

68

it was me with the problem; *do I mumble?* I knew I often forgot to do things, so maybe I had other issues with how I communicated, too. Once I bought a roast and put it in the refrigerator. I told Garry, "There's a roast in there. Don't let me forget to cook it." Garry: "There's a roach in the refrigerator, and you want to cook it?"

One night I was watching *American Idol*, and I told Garry, who was working on his computer, "That guy is from Bremen." To that, he looked up and said, "How do you know he's been drinking?"

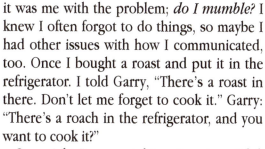

Once when we were traveling late at night and eating popcorn to stay awake I told him, "You're going to need another toothpick after this." He answered, "No, I'm okay. I peed before we left." On that same note, we were eating lunch out one day, and I told Garry, "I dropped a pea on myself!" He said to me, "Can't you make it to the bathroom?" I asked, "Why?" He answered, "Maybe you can get to the bathroom before you pee on yourself." One day I looked down at my chipped nail and said, "Oh, this THING!" Garry said, "You think I stink?" I got home from a walk one day, and I told Garry, "Well, I got rained on." He said, "You got ringworm???" "No, RAINED on!" Garry, relieved, said, "Well, that's a whole lot easier to take care of than ringworm!"

I'll have to admit there was at least one incident when I didn't understand what he was saying to me. One cold, winter night we were called to the hospital by a church member; while we were waiting outside of the ER, I

told Garry I was cold. He looked down at me and said sweetly, "Do you want to make love?" I looked at our friend Melinda, who was with us, and she had heard it as I did. She was shocked that her pastor would say such a thing. Then I responded to Garry, "Well, not right now—maybe later!" He had actually asked me, "Do you want my gloves?"

For me, the most beautiful things in life are not things, after all. *But God* gives us people and moments and smiles and laughter.

He may not hear everything I say, but I'm so thankful for the man I get to live with, laugh with, and love. God knew just what I needed, and He gave me Garry.

Chapter 28

I will always wonder why bad things happen to good people. Nobody is exempt. Life happens, and it's not always what we have planned. That's why Jeremiah 29:11 was a verse that spoke to me loudly during the next season of my life. *"For I know the plans I have for you," says the Lord. "They are plans for good and not for disaster to give you a future and a hope."*

In the summer of 2012, Mom was diagnosed with breast cancer. I couldn't believe it, and I was devastated. She was 87 years old. We sought out many opinions about what to do. We ended up at the University of Tennessee Medical Center, and Mom loved the surgeon. He was not good-looking, but he was a University of Alabama graduate. When he found out that she was a fan, he said, "Wow! Roll Damn Tide!" When he asked her if she smoked, she said, "No." "Do you drink?" "No, I don't CUSS either!"

Even though he cussed, she still liked him and decided that she would trust him to perform a mastectomy. He assured her that he had never lost anyone doing this surgery. So I think he was just as shocked as we were when he came out of the surgery and told us she had flat-lined before the surgery had even begun. They revived her, but her life as we knew it was never the same after that day.

Because Mom was in a very weakened state, we needed to move her into a rehab center. We quickly discovered that our best option was to move her to Birmingham, Alabama, where our family lived. Stephanie, our niece, was HR Director for a health services corporation, and she got Mom a room at the perfect place. I will always believe that God used Stephanie to bless us at that time.

We thought the stay at the rehab facility was temporary. So, when our son Greg asked us to be guests in their home, we were so very thankful. Mom was less than ten minutes away from us.

Our last family Christmas in the Mountain House, December 2011

Our lives completely changed during that time, *But God* held us, and we knew we were never alone. Little did we know that our most devastating days were ahead.

Chapter 29

Our granddaughter Kayla left Birmingham in January of 2013 for Hawaii to prepare for a three-month mission trip to a country to be decided later. We were so proud of her, and we knew she would be a beautiful Voice for the Voiceless wherever God sent her.

After her orientation and training, she arrived in Kenya, Africa. Sadly, she only stayed a short time because she began having frequent nose bleeds and unexplained bruising. It was decided that she should return home. When I saw her at the Atlanta Airport, I knew she was very sick, but I was so not prepared to find out what had been causing her health problems.

Austin and Kayla at her high school graduation party

Not long after her return home, we were told that our 18-year-old granddaughter had cancer—more specifically, 90 percent of her bone marrow was covered in cancer. She had stage 4 Neuroblastoma, a childhood cancer. Had she stayed in Africa, she probably would not have made it.

Kayla in Kenya

To say we were heartbroken is an understatement. We were still living with Greg when he came home and told me the news. He didn't have to tell me; it was evident from the tears in his eyes. Garry was in Guatemala, and Greg and Lee Anne let me call him from their phone. We cried together, and we felt so helpless and afraid. It was devastating to even think about. Lee Anne prayed the sweetest prayer with me, and thankfully, the volunteer team

from the Church at Liberty Park prayed with Garry. Many times in the months ahead, I asked, *"But God, WHY?"* It was something I could never understand. Kayla's journey with cancer was so difficult for me to watch. Her faith was strong, though, and the prayers and support of literally thousands of people most certainly got us through each day.

For our family, it was the most bittersweet thing we had ever gone through together. One of the sweetest times for us happened at the beginning of Kayla's treatment. She was losing her hair, and she knew she needed to shave it off. So, her boyfriend Austin, her dad Rob, her brother Andrew, and her cousins Samuel, Michael, Daniel, and Jared, decided to get together and shave their heads along with Kayla. Those were the most beautiful bald heads I had ever seen. A few days later, Kayla took toboggans to each one of them so their heads wouldn't get cold. Even in her pain, she was always thinking of others.

From the ends of the earth, I cry to you for help when my heart is overwhelmed. Lead me to the towering rock of safety,

Psalms 61:2

74

Chapter 30

During those not so-normal-days, life still happened. Garry's trips to Guatemala became more frequent as more volunteer teams began to go there for ministry. He happened to leave on Valentine's Day on one of those trips. He called me that night and told me where he had left me my card. I found it and then I told him, "I put yours in your suitcase." He responded, "You put mine in my toothpaste?!" Yep, right where he would see it when he brushed his teeth.

Mom's visits with Morgan were always fun

On another occasion, early one morning when Garry was supposed to leave for the airport in a taxi, he woke me up suddenly. The taxi had not come, and he needed me to take him to the airport—immediately! I didn't even have time to get dressed. I wasn't really worried, because all I had to do was leave him at the outside gate and come home. After I dropped him off, I drove toward the airport exit. I looked down and saw that he had left his telephone on the dashboard. "Oh, no!" I said out loud to myself, "I need to call him and tell him he left his phone!" Well, duh! I couldn't call him! I was going to have to take the phone to him before he went through customs. So, I parked the car, got out, and ran for about two blocks on the sidewalk. I entered the airport, ran up to the counter where he was checking in, and put his phone down. Then I ran back to the car as fast as I could and got in. On the way home, I talked to the Lord and told Him that I hoped no one noticed me in my pajamas! It was a crazy thing that I did, *But God* knew I needed to hear Garry's voice on the phone each night he was in Guatemala. The stories he told of how God was changing lives there were simply amazing.

Kayla, Morgan, Me, Christen, and Mom

While he was on that trip, he called me on one of those nights, and I could tell he was very emotional. He had just preached to 150 pastors, and he shared with them about Kayla. Before they left, all of them gathered around him and prayed for her and our family. God was there, and He ministered to Garry in a beautiful way.

My days were mostly filled spending time with Mom at the rehabilitation center. Our family was very supportive and helpful. My sweet sister-in-law Anne spent every Friday with her, giving me a needed break. Mama looked forward to her visits from our kids and grandkids. Her caregivers there were exceptional, and she made lots of friends. She made sure that everyone who prayed, prayed for Kayla. It made me so sad to see her in the condition she was in. She was now in a wheelchair all the time.

She and I had some sweet times when we talked about God and Heaven and our lives here on earth. She even talked about her drunk daddy raping her as a child and how she dealt with it as an adult. Obviously, it was devastating and traumatic, but she had chosen to forgive him—even though he had never asked or even acknowledged the heinous act. She told me that she wanted to be better, not bitter; she knew that not forgiving him did more to hurt her than it did him. I could see the sadness and pain in her eyes when she talked, and it

Mom and granddaughter Laurie

Mom's favorite caregiver Delores

Mom's Best friend Glenda

made me sick. But I was so proud of her for choosing not to stay in that pit of unforgiveness.

Mom, Garry, and I had a very unique worship experience while she was there. When we arrived to visit with her one Sunday morning, Garry was asked to share a message with a group who had gathered for

Mom loved her Friday visits with Anne

Mom loved her visits with Garry's sister Kathy

Greg's family with Mom

Grant's family with Mom, Nancy, and me

their church service. It was an unusual crowd. Some were very alert, but sadly, others didn't even know where they were. At the beginning of his message, Garry sang a verse of *Beautiful Star of Bethlehem*. His sermon was about how Jesus, the Beautiful Star, is always with us and never leaves us no matter where we are or what our circumstances are. That message spoke to me, even if it didn't touch another soul.

>   *...be kind to each other, tenderhearted, forgiving one another, just as God through Christ has forgiven you.*
>
>   Ephesians 4:32

Chapter 31

Mom never really got any better physically. In fact, she got progressively worse. She was taken to the hospital on several occasions because of heart issues. On one of those occasions, I arrived early in the morning to see her. She began telling me that she didn't get any sleep the night before because loud music was being played while the nurses and doctors made love all night. She was convinced that the dietitian was Rudolph, the Red-nosed Reindeer and that Garry had come to visit her with a wig on. That visit with her was very interesting.

After both visits to the hospital, she improved and went back "home," as she had started calling the nursing home. So, I didn't think the third time would be any different. That's why, in the early hours of February 13, 2014, I was surprised when I got a call from her CICU nurse who told me she didn't think Mom would live through the night. I really couldn't believe it. I had just seen her the day before, and she seemed fine. I had to say goodbye to her earlier than usual that evening because a snowstorm was coming, and I needed to get home.

The trip to the hospital that morning on snow and ice-covered roads was treacherous, *But God* protected us, and we arrived around 2:00 a.m. at her room. Almost immediately upon seeing Mom, I could tell the situation wasn't good. Moments later I received a Facebook message from our friend Ingrid, in Guatemala. She told me that God had awakened her and put on her heart to pray for us. I began to cry and couldn't even see to answer her message, so I handed my phone to Garry. He told her our situation, and she assured us that she and her husband Otto were praying.

We strongly felt God's presence in that room as we sat by Mom's bed. Garry sang hymns to her and prayed with her. All I could do was talk to her and cry. I felt like she knew we were there, although she never responded. I was holding her hand when, at 6:00 a.m., she slipped into the arms of Jesus. I had to say goodbye to the one who had led me to faith in Christ and the one who, I'm sure, was my greatest prayer support throughout my life. It was a hard good-bye because I needed to talk to her about so much more. *But God* gave us a beautiful Hope that one day we would see my mama, my daddy, my brother, and all our other loved ones who had gone to be with Jesus before that day. That assurance gave me such comfort and peace.

I pray that God, the source of hope, will fill you completely with joy and peace because you trust in him. Then you will overflow with confident hope through the power of the Holy Spirit.

Romans 15:13

Chapter 32

In the months before and after Mom's death, we watched Kayla suffer throughout her battle with cancer. She had received a full scholarship to Auburn University but couldn't go because she was so sick. Her new normal consisted of chemo, numerous blood and platelet transfusions, bone marrow biopsies, high fevers, terrible pain, nausea, vomiting, mouth sores, clinic visits, a stem cell transplant, radiation, and multiple hospital admissions. Much of the time, she was so sick she couldn't even hold her head up. Sometimes we had hope, only to be devastated by another setback. It was after one of those relapses that she decided, with the advice of her doctor, to go on with her life—because there was no cure for her cancer. So she packed up in the fall of 2014 and headed to Auburn to begin classes.

After Kayla had been in Auburn a few days, Kayla's dad Rob felt God leading him to go to Auburn and visit with her. Even though the doctor indicated that cancer could take Kayla's life, Rob wanted to encourage her to fight and not give up. And giving up was the last thing on Kayla's mind. She had goals and dreams. She

The Perry family

wanted to LIVE until she died. That night at dinner, among other things, Rob and Kayla talked about Joshua on the night before he crossed the Jordan River and marched around the city of Jericho. God's instructions truly made no sense. *But God* told Joshua to be strong and very courageous and assured him that He was with him wherever he went. So Joshua crossed into enemy territory only with faithful obedience. Rob encouraged Kayla to do the same.

Rob wrote these words soon after that visit, "Kayla stands at the same spot and is marching ahead on her journey and is looking to her Savior for deliverance. No matter the journey, the struggle, or the odds, we will continue to trust and cry out to God to do more than we can ever hope or imagine. With God, all things are possible."

During that year, Kayla traveled once a week from Auburn to Atlanta for treatments. She started a non-profit organization, Open Hands Overflowing Hearts, to raise awareness and funds for childhood cancer research.

Kayla with Auburn alum, Uncles Grant and Greg

Unbelievably, she also made all *As* in her classes. Joshua 1:7 *Be strong and Very Courageous* became the verse she claimed for herself and so many other children fighting for their lives.

Austin, Kayla, Coach Malzahn, and Rob

Aubie was a fan

None of us knew how much time Kayla had left on this earth, but we knew she was fighting hard, her faith in the Lord was strong, and she had literally thousands of people praying for her healing. Even with that, it was the hardest thing in the world to watch her suffer. And it was a struggle for us not to be afraid and discouraged.

But God was with our family, holding us, carrying us, and loving us. We were never alone.

Jesus looked at them intently and said, "Humanly speaking, it is impossible. But not with God. Everything is possible with God."

Mark 10:27

Chapter 33

During those dark days, I not only got strength from God but also from my family and friends. Kayla had a CaringBridge web page, and her mom Christen would share prayer needs, encouraging messages, scripture, and songs. Both of our sons, Grant and Greg, are doctors. They understood when I needed to talk or just be with them and their families. Garry's brother Jack and his wife Debbie created prayer bracelets for everyone who wanted to be reminded to pray for Kayla. Kathy, Garry's sister, helped Kayla design a t-shirt that said, "Cancer Doesn't Scare God" on the front, and on the back, Psalms 91:2, *This I declare about the Lord. He alone is my Refuge, my place of safety; He is my God and I trust Him.* Those bracelets and t-shirts gave us all opportunities to share Kayla's story and ask for prayer.

Even on the worst days, I experienced some of the sweetest times of my life with Kayla's brother Andrew, our oldest grandson. I don't know why he wanted to spend time with me, but I felt the love. He would take me on hikes through a nature preserve near our house or along the river, where he would swing from a

limb and drop into the river. At times he would take me to the top of one of the highest points above Birmingham, and we would just sit and talk and look down onto the beautiful skyline and the Children's Hospital of Alabama where Kayla was. Then we would go for lunch or ice cream. Sometimes we would go to the mall, and I would buy him soccer shoes. Those trips may have cost me, but Andrew's hugs, smiles, and the times spent with him were priceless. Who would have thought I so needed those hugs? *But God*, during those stormy days, used hugs from Andrew to show His love for me, over and over again.

Our friends were also amazing. Their prayers for Kayla and for us brought me such comfort. Our Bible study class at Hunter Street Baptist faithfully prayed for her and our family. They loved on us every Sunday.

Sheryl, one of our special friends in Douglasville, Georgia, raised $5,000 for Kayla's foundation by getting the girls in her dance studio to dance!

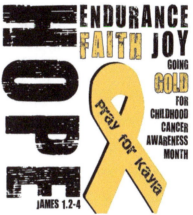

Several times Garry and I made trips back to our mountain house in Tennessee. On one of those occasions, our friends Joan and Sam asked us to meet them at our church there, Valley View Baptist in Wears Valley. They placed their hands on us and prayed for Kayla's healing and our family. Those were some of the most precious moments I've ever spent in prayer.

On one occasion, Kayla, even though she was sick, just wanted to get away and enjoy some time with her friends, and we told them to go to our mountain house. Two precious friends from the church, Sheila and Paula, lovingly stocked the refrigerator and cabinets with everything they would need during their visit. I can't imagine going through life, much less heartache, without such loving friends.

Kayla herself was also such an inspiration to me, as she frequently blogged throughout her journey. This entry was one of many that encouraged me during the darkest of days:

Dear Kayla,

I am holding you in My arms. I know you're scared, but you don't have to be. I am working all things together for good. I didn't call you to do this alone. You have an army of prayer warriors standing behind you, and, of course, you have me. You are weak; let me be your strength. You are exhausted; let me be your energy. You are hurting; let me be your comfort. You are afraid; let me be your Peace. You don't have to ask me to carry your burdens because I'm already carrying them. All you have to do is quit trying to do it yourself. I'm taking care of you, and I have a plan for your life. I know it doesn't make much sense to you right now, and I know you are confused, but I am looking at the big picture, and it all makes perfect sense to me. I'm sorry you have to go through this. You know, I hate cancer. I hate to see my children suffer. But that's part of the curse that was placed on this earth when Adam and Eve sinned. My people will continue to suffer until I come back and make a New Heaven and a New Earth. But as much as I hate that you have to go through this, I love that you are learning to walk by faith and totally rely on me. My power is made perfect in your weakness. There are so many things going on right now that you can't see, but someday, I'll let you sit in my lap while I show you all the things I'm doing in your life right now. I love you, my sweet, precious daughter. Sweet dreams.

Love,
God

Even during her worst days, Kayla never stopped thinking of other children with cancer. Each February, she encouraged us to give up something and give to research to find a cure. She, herself, would always give up something, also. During one of her setbacks, she  wrote this: "Here we are on February 5th, and I've already given up so much more than coffee. I gave up my ability to walk without a walker and drive a car. Worst of all, I gave up my ability to go to school this semester. But what I haven't given up is this: Hope. I'm ready to push through this setback, just like I've pushed through every single one before. With the Father by my side, gently nudging me from behind, holding my hands, He whispers to me that He has not left me alone."

... For God has said, "I will never fail you. I will never abandon you."
Hebrews 13:5b

Chapter 34

The summer after Mom's death I had an opportunity to go back to Guatemala with several volunteer teams. Truthfully, I didn't know if I should go or not. Fear, the liar, reared his ugly head again. What if something happened while I was so far away? I was talking to Kayla about it, and I told her that I probably wouldn't go. She told me, "Why wouldn't you go, Tita? You should go! If I could go, I would!" Those words made me know I had to go. If I hadn't gone, I'd have missed so many blessings.

Samuel and Michael's forever friends in Guatemala

I would have missed our grandson Samuel say to his new friends in San Juan La Laguna, "I've loved playing basketball with you this week, but I came here to tell you about the best thing that has ever happened to me." Then, as I translated for him, he used a visual aid called an *Evangecube* to share the Gospel with them. That day, each one of those boys prayed and asked Jesus to be their Savior. They all became our forever friends, and even now, we love on each other when we go back to San Juan.

I would have also missed watching our granddaughter Morgan, along with a team from our former church, Central Baptist, lovingly teach Bible stories to the children. Oh, how they loved Morgan's beautiful, long blonde hair and her sweet hugs. The soccer stadium, full of students, became totally silent as she shared about her relationship with Jesus and how He was strengthening her faith as she was walking through dark days as a "cancer sister" to Kayla. At one of our medical clinics, I got to watch her work in triage and love on sweet little babies and their mommies. It was a precious sight!

I also got to watch our grandsons Michael and Jared, in San Andres, El Peten, running around in the hottest place in Guatemala playing soccer with the school children. When they stopped to rest, they would use the colors on the soccer ball to share Jesus with them.

On several trips, I got to see both of our sons and other doctors treat literally thousands of patients who otherwise wouldn't have been able to afford medical care. Our medical clinics also gave out medicine and eyeglasses. Every person who saw a doctor got to hear the Gospel and had an opportunity to follow Jesus.

So many hearts were changed, including mine. I knew I would never be the same after my trips to Guatemala that year and the next. At first, I was hesitant to go, *But God* knew I needed to see Him work, more than anything.

Therefore, God elevated him to the place of highest honor, and gave him the name above all other names, that at the name of Jesus every knee should bow, in heaven and on earth and under the earth, and every tongue declare that Jesus Christ is Lord, to the glory of God the Father.
Philippians 2:9-11

Morgan with her little students

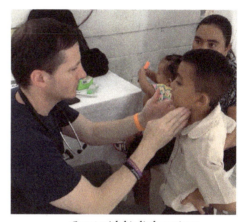

Grant with his little patients

Garry sharing the Gospel with the students

Michael and Pastor Scott praying with a patient after sharing the Gospel

Morgan throwing an American Football into the soccer net

Garry preaching to the students

Samuel and Denis squaring off

Jared and a new friend

He followed Morgan everywhere

Morgan loved the babies

Everybody loved Morgan

Chapter 35

I will never forget the morning of November 7, 2015. It was the beginning of some of the most difficult days of my life. I was in Douglasville, Georgia, about to speak at a women's ministry event at our former church, Central Baptist. I was so excited about being with and sharing my heart with some of the most beautiful women I knew. Before I left my bed and breakfast at my friend Bonnie's house, I received a phone call from Kayla. She was in the middle of a huge battle with her cancer. In May, she had to have brain surgery because a tumor had been found on her brain stem. That morning in November, she called me with the disturbing news that scans had shown two more brain tumors. How could I even speak, much less stand before a group of women and encourage them? *But God*, more than ever, gave me the strength to get through that day. He spoke through me, but I received so much needed love, encouragement, and prayers for Kayla and our family. He loved on me that day in the most extraordinary way through my forever friends. God's Love Wins. Every. Time.

The doctors hoped that radiation would take care of Kayla's tumors, but sadly, it did not. So, in January of 2016, the tumors were removed once again. We had hope that surgery would be the answer, but, tragically, in early February, the tumors came back. The family was told there was nothing else that could be done and that Kayla had maybe six to eight weeks to live.

Kayla was asked what was the one thing she really wanted to do, and she said, "I want to marry Austin!" Austin had been Kayla's boyfriend since high school and had already lovingly and faithfully chosen to help her throughout her journey and even during her worst days. They were obviously very much in love. So on April 2nd he got down on one knee at the beach and asked Kayla to be his wife. The wedding was already being planned—because timing was everything.

Kayla's mom Christen, who owns her own travel business, planned an amazing destination wedding at the British island territory of Turks and Caicos for May 21. Family and a few friends arrived, not knowing what to expect. *But God* gave Kayla and Austin the best day ever.

As beautiful Kayla walked down the ramp of the sandy beach toward the ocean, Austin turned to look at her. He began to sob; the tears were literally streaming down his face. When Kayla reached him, she placed her hands on his face and wiped away his tears. By this time, all of us were crying. The memories of that perfect day will always and forever be in my mind and heart. None of us really knew how much more time Kayla had or what the future held, *But God* did. All we knew to do was trust Him.

I will cast all my cares on you, Lord, and you will take care of me.
As for me I trust in you.

Psalm 55:22 (my personal paraphrase)

Chapter 36

So, what do you do during uncertain days when you really have no idea what's next? You just keep following God down the path He has you on. For us, the path was often dark, *But God* was the Light in our darkness. Jesus said, *I am the Light of the world. If you follow me, you won't have to walk in darkness, because you will have the light that leads to life.* John 8:12. So many things happened during those days that we were not expecting.

God showed us during that time that He was working in Guatemala more than we could've ever imagined or hoped for. The number of teams going there from the U.S. was growing each year. The Tennessee Baptist Mission Board had partnered with E3 Volunteers. They, along with churches in Alabama, Georgia, Florida, and South Carolina, were taking teams to Guatemala to partner

Otto and Ruth Echeveria and Otto and Ingrid Castañon with us at the 35th Anniversary of Partnership Missions in TN

Our E3 Partners Sheila and Marty Dodge and Richard Lewelling, visited with us at our table

Garry about to preach at our partner church, with Pastor Glen Metts

Jeanne and Randy Davis, Executive Director of TN Baptist Convention, and Salvador Zapeta, President of Guatemala Baptist

Mario and Leticia Garcia were our guests

with churches and communities all over the country. We were taking vision, medical, sports, children's education, and construction teams. Many people were finding Hope in Jesus and, at the same time, their physical needs were being met. Every time I went, God worked, once again, in my own heart.

Incredibly, the President of Guatemala heard about our work and asked to meet with Garry and some pastors who were working alongside us. None of us could have ever dreamed up that meeting. *But God* made it happen. The President expressed his appreciation for what E3 was doing and asked us if we could take teams to remote towns and villages to work in their schools. One of those places was a very remote village close to the border of Mexico.

Garry, Guatemalan President Jimmy Morales, First Lady Patricia Marroquin, Omar, Alvaro, Otto, and Jose Angel

Soon after that meeting with the president, Garry and some of our dear Guatemalan friends visited that village. They didn't know this, *But God* was already at work there. The group came upon a rustic building that looked like it could be a church; and indeed, it was a church. The pastor of that church had come to the United States as a young man, and while he was here, he gave his heart to Jesus. Soon afterward, he felt God calling him to preach, so he attended a Bible school. He felt God telling him to go back home to his village in Guatemala and share the Gospel with his people. He then went back home and started a church. Before Garry went to the village, no one even knew he was there. *But God* had put him there in San Andres Huista, and he was so ready to partner with us. That's what I call a God story.

Mario, David, Greg, Randy, Bruce, Me, Garry, William, and Salvador outside the National Palace in Guatemala after meeting with First Lady, Patricia Marroquin

Construction Team from Central

Central's Medical, Construction, and Children's Team

Central's James and Jason

Construction Team from Central

Construction Team from Central, Douglasville, GA

Bruce and Mike with the 1st Baptist Hendersonville, TN Team

Student Team from Shades Mountain Baptist, Birmingham, AL

Team from First Baptist Church Villa Rica, GA

Chapter 37

I definitely wasn't prepared for what I saw when I first went to San Andres Huista with a team from Shades Mountain Baptist Church. We traveled twelve hours in the mountain highlands to get to the town we where we stayed. The village was an hour from our hotel, and we traveled there on a curvy, muddy, mountainous road. Someone told us that it had been over twenty years since the villagers had seen a white person. Some were, at first, obviously afraid of us. The poverty there was indescribable. I imagined that it had been awhile since some of them had had any kind of medical attention. Hundreds lined up to see our doctors. I watched as our son Greg, a rheumatologist, took vials of liquid from the legs of a woman with rheumatoid arthritis. She had nowhere to live, and we eventually built her a house using generous donations from friends. There was a little boy who had never seen clearly until he was given glasses by our eye doctor. I cried when I saw his sweet, thankful smile.

Before we even arrived, hundreds were waiting to see our two doctors

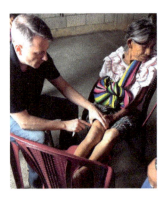

The beauty of the school children took my breath away. They didn't speak Spanish; their language was Popti, so the only language they could understand was Love. Never in my life have I seen so much love shown: Samuel began bouncing balloons up in the air, and all the kids began to do the same; Michael jumped and sang and shouted nonsensical words that nobody understood but copied anyway; Daniel made up games and played whiffle ball with them; our boys carried the little guys on their backs and endlessly swung them around. Their laughter and smiles melted my heart. When we left the worksite, they climbed trees so they could wave goodbye to us.

Every afternoon we invited the children and their parents to join us at the church. The crowds grew by the hundreds each day as word spread that we were there. Our team of young people played soccer and other games with the kids on the dirt floor of the church. Then they sang songs with them and told them Bible stories. I couldn't stop taking pictures of their precious faces.

After the kids and their parents left, some of the older women of the church took water, sprinkled it on the dirt floor, and swept it with a broom. That broke my heart. It must have broken another team member's heart, too, because the next year when we went back, he had donated money for a concrete floor. His donation was also used to install a water filtration system at the school so the kids could have clean water to drink. Sadly, there was no solution for the only way to flush the toilet—dip into a container of river water and pour it in.

Even though the church was not beautiful, one of the most beautiful events I've ever witnessed happened there. I got to see our grandson Michael preach his first sermon in Guatemala. His passion for others to know Christ inspired me. I

Michael's first sermon, with Damaris interpreting for him into Spanish and Pastor Felipe interpreting into Popti

knew God had a plan like no other for his life. It was then that God reminded me again—this was one of the reasons He had called me to be a missionary so many years before.

So now I am giving you a new commandment: Love each other. Just as I have loved you, you should love each other. Your love for one another will prove to the world that you are my disciples.

John 13:34-35

School Director thanking Garry for their first water filtration system.

After school hundreds of kids showed up at church for games, songs, and Bible stories

Chapter 38

Wow—as a young adult, I thought I had my life all figured out. *But God* had a plan for me and my family that was greater than anything I could have ever imagined. The blessings just kept coming.

I could never have imagined that one morning I would wake up in a Guatemalan hotel listening to the cutest, most musically talented guy singing *This Is Amazing Grace* in the shower. Oh yes! God let me experience that precious moment with my roommate, grandson Daniel, after I had been on a mission team with him, his mom Lee Anne, his dad Greg, and his brother Samuel.

I saw many new houses being built for people who previously lived in deplorable, unsafe conditions. Neighbors came for the dedication of the houses and heard the Gospel presented. Many came to know the Lord, and they knew that those houses were gifts from God.

I watched a beautiful church building go up in San Juan La Laguna because Dr. Kevin Williams, pastor of First Baptist Church Villa Rica, Ga., had a vision of planting a church there. Then Kevin baptized new believers year after year in the beautiful Lake Atitlan. One year they left their footprints behind by leaving 150 pairs of shoes for the children there. Every year they have sponsored dozens of school children so they can continue their education. So many lives, including children, parents, directors, and teachers, have been changed forever by God. The amazing thing is that Kevin keeps looking for other places around the lake to work. He's even taken other pastors from

My roommate Daniel and I riding a Tuk-tuk

Eudy family: Greg, Lee Anne, Daniel, Samuel, and Michael— Capuchinas, Antigua, Guatemala after serving in San Juan, La Laguna.

Kevin and his beautiful wife Patrice with us in San Juan, La Laguna

Pastor Kevin baptizing in Lake Atitlan with Garry interpreting

Georgia and encouraged them to begin work there—and they have!

I watched men from The Church at Liberty Park and Locust Fork Baptist Church build a house for a pastor and his wife to live in while starting a church. Every year, that same group of men worked on renovating bathrooms, painting classrooms, and putting a new roof on the school. They also built a house for an elderly couple; he's blind, and she is diabetic. Their mud house had been condemned. Now they have a block home and a wood-burning oven that is ventilated. They no longer have to breathe damaging smoke every time they cook.

In San Andres, El Peten, I saw one of our doctors purchase a wheelchair for a woman who had no legs. One of our young team members lifted her up, and with tears in his eyes, placed her gently into her new chair. She didn't have to crawl on her hands anymore.

I watched as Michael gave a Bible to his new little friend Jesus, who stood alone in his classroom and asked Jesus Christ into his life. He had never received such a gift before!

Liberty Park and Locust Fork Baptist churches' construction teams raising a house's walls in El Peten

Liberty Park and Locust Fork Baptist churches' construction teams building a house for a local elderly couple in San Andres, El Peten, Guatemala

Jared's Soccer Ball Ministry is always a big hit with the kiddos

I listened as Samuel and Michael passionately talked to a group of students who had just asked Jesus into their lives. They explained to them how to grow as Christians. And no, that time they no longer needed me to translate. Their Spanish was incredible!

I watched as 6'5" Cameron, our future grandson-in-law, put kids on his shoulders so they could dunk the basketball. And then he lovingly helped them learn how to hold and swing a bat. Oh, the looks on their faces!

I listened as Samuel shared his story about struggling with depression with a group of students. A little guy, Miguel Jesus, found him afterward and told him that he was very sad and

had thought about ending his own life. The image of Samuel sitting with Miguel and assuring him that his life WAS worth living will forever be on my mind. Samuel shared with him how Jesus could change his life, and Miguel wanted that. That day he chose Jesus and Life! Samuel has been back to visit him several times since then, and the little man is so happy; he told Samuel that he thinks about Jesus and Samuel all the time!

I watched as Kaylee, our youngest grandchild, helped her mom Shelley work in the classroom with adoring kids her age. She loved handing out crayons and craft material and working with them on projects. Those kids loved her, and she loved them right back!

I was with Morgan as she gently placed reading glasses on Elena, a precious 90-year-old woman. Then Morgan opened the Bible to John 3:16 and asked Elena to read it. It was a beautiful God moment.

I watched at the airport as a woman approached our son Grant and asked him to buy something from her so she could buy her child an inhaler. She had no idea he was a doctor and that he had inhalers with him. He reached into his bag and gave her one. She just kept on saying, over and over, "God bless you! God bless you!"

I had the privilege of meeting a guy named Carlos; he had left Guatemala and lived in Los Angeles for many years. While he was there, he was a drug user, a drug dealer, and a gang member. He eventually managed to leave the United States and return to Guatemala. His kids wanted so much for him to give up his alcohol and drugs, and they convinced him to go to church with them. One of our teams from

Tennessee was there that day, and they told him about Jesus. He gave his life to the Lord and was changed forever! He later translated for us on one of my trips. God used him to minister to us as well as the beautiful children he encouraged on the way.

I watched as a school building was built from vacation Bible school offerings taken at First Baptist Church, Hendersonville, TN. Before the school was built, the kids attended school in a dirt floor shed.

Because of a generous donation from some dear friends, I was able to see a water project—bringing good water from a mile above a rural town to the homes below—begun. The villagers now have clean water to drink.

I listened as Garry told me about a sports team he was with from Tennessee. They played basketball with at-risk kids all week. After the clinic, eight of them were changed forever as they asked Christ into their lives!

Church at Liberty Park and 1st Baptist Locust Fork Teams

I got to be with Grant and Shelley as they celebrated their 21st Anniversary in Guatemala. He saw patients while she worked with children. Their kids and the team celebrated with them all day long. It was simply beautiful!

Each time I go to Guatemala, I just want to be a blessing by loving on and helping the precious people there. *But God* has given me so many blessings in return. I'm sure that the thousands of other volunteers who have gone with us feel the same. Truly, good things come to those who care, share, and go.

Now all glory to God, who is able, through his mighty power at work within us, to accomplish infinitely more than we might ask or think.

Ephesians 3:20

Chapter 39

I must admit that many of my visits to Guatemala are just not normal. On one trip, I almost got electrocuted in the shower when I accidentally touched the electrically powered hot water contraption—yes, the infamous widow-maker. In my case, it would have made Garry a widower.

I've also had several encounters with lizards. Once, one decided to jump into my hair. Then another night when I got into the bed, one decided to drop down from the ceiling light into my bed right next to me. Both times I let out a loud scream.

On another trip, I almost missed my flight out of Birmingham because TSA mistook my hot rollers for a bomb, of all things. That same morning, I did the splits several times, running down the hallway toward the boarding gate while trying to manage my luggage. I needed my traveling partner, but he was already in Guatemala.

Then there was the time after arriving in Atlanta from Guatemala when my grandkids watched as I was detained and frisked. It seems that the carrot bread in my carry-on smelled like drugs. And of course, I must have looked like a drug-smuggling terrorist instead of a grandmother returning home from a mission trip with her grandkids!

I may get a little crazy, too, while I'm there. I've been known to hang out with the FBI or get on a scooter or two. I don't know what it is about being in Guatemala, but our boys, even in their late 40s, like to turn flips at beautiful Lake Atitlan!

I had one bittersweet experience. I didn't know it, but I had contracted pneumonia, probably before my trip to the hottest place in El Peten, Guatemala. I struggled all week, and I felt pretty useless. I was too sick to go to the worksite, and my sweet grandson Jared would bring meals to my room—I was being served rather than serving. On the last day, our doctors were attending to our hotel employees right outside my room. I was resting when Michael knocked on my door. "Tita, Come quickly! I need you to translate!" I got outside, and

Nancy and I hanging with the FBI in Panajachel, Solola, Guatemala

Grant flipping at San Marcos, La Laguna, Lake Atitlan

Greg flipping high above Lake Atitlan

Michael was sharing about Christ with one of our servers who, we discovered, had never heard the Gospel. After a few minutes of translating, I began coughing, and I knew what was coming. "Michael, I need to throw-up!" So, I went into my room, threw up, and got back outside as quickly as I could. We continued. The sweet part of that day is that our beautiful server's life was changed forever as she asked Jesus to come into her life. I was sick, Michael needed help with his Spanish, *But God* used us anyway. That was one blessing I didn't see coming.

106

With Grant in a Tuk-tuk, my favorite ride

Watching Greg's Titanic Pose on a lancha

T-Shirt: "Every day I wake up handsome, but today I exaggerated!"

Chapter 40

I should have known that God was about to do something special when we arrived at the Birmingham Airport early on the morning of June 1, 2018. Garry was already in Guatemala, and Samuel, Michael, and I were on our way to stay for a month. When we sat down at the gate, God allowed us to meet Ryan, a young man who had just been released from rehab for abusing alcohol and drugs. We got to encourage him, pray with him, and buy him a few snacks. Little did we know, but that was the first of many God encounters we would have that month. Michael was so excited, he wrote a beautiful poem:

Hi Ho, Hi Ho, Hi Ho. Off for a month, I go.
And when I return, in my heart it will burn,
This fire for the Lord, I couldn't ask for more.
So, Guatemala, here I come. Lord let Your will be done,
Because Jesus, my Father, my Savior, my King,
The Ruler of everything,
You are my One desire; I lift no other name higher.
So, I will share Your Name, and God I'll spread Your fame
To family, to friends, and to nations afar.
Jesus, wherever You lead me, I give You my heart.

Waiting to board our flight at the Birmingham Airport with Michael, Samuel, Hannah, and Mary Beth

The fact was that we were all excited, but we got worried when our flight out of Birmingham to Atlanta kept getting delayed. We finally landed in Atlanta at the exact moment our plane was scheduled to take off for Guatemala. To say we ran is an understatement—some of us ran faster than others.

Samuel and Michael arrived at the gate and literally begged the gate attendants to wait for me and the girls who were with me. At first, they refused; but the boys kept asking and explaining why they should wait. When they saw us rounding the corner, they waited for us to board before they shut the gate. It was a miracle that we got on that flight.

When I boarded the plane, I was so relieved that I shouted, "Woo Hoo!" Well, that was a mistake. The flight attendant approached me and told me I was

Michael and Samuel headed to Team Worship

Samuel is known for his epic brushing of teeth for long periods of time.

disturbing the other passengers. She probably didn't know that over half of the passengers, 68 to be exact, were on our volunteer team and were glad to see me. At any rate, she asked me if I had been drinking. "No, I'm a preacher's wife." She looked down at me and said, "Well, then, you should know better." I apologized and found my seat, so happy not to have been thrown from the airplane. Samuel was not too happy with her, because she had no idea what getting on that plane meant to us.

Hopewell Baptist Church Team from Canton, Georgia

Third week of our mission trip in Morales

First Baptist Villa Rica, GA Team waiting for the lancha to cross Lake Atitlan, Guatemala

Chapter 41

That month with our summer missionaries—Samuel, Michael, Anna, Morgan, Elayna, Maggie, and Sophia—was one of the most incredible months I've ever spent in my lifetime. I got to watch some of the most God-loving high school and college students serve the Lord and love on the Guatemalans. And they all called me Tita.

So, what made that month with those young people so special for me? Of course, it was the God appointments, the sweet sound of worship at night in our hotels, the prayers, the smiles, the laughs, the fun, the bonding with each other, and especially the name of Jesus being lifted up and shared every day.

Michael with his little friend Jesus

It was watching them play and work and love on the precious kids. It was watching as they prayed with and gave money to an old handicapped man so he could buy new shoes. It was the air-drop parties every night. It was watching Samuel and Michael use their own money to buy one of their friends a pair of shoes for his birthday. It was the joy of knowing what a difference God was making in each of their lives and how He was working out His plan for them.

It was being a part of four different mission teams and seeing over one thousand people come to know Jesus as their Lord and Savior. It was being so blessed—not just being a blessing.

And finally, it was being amazed as I watched Michael preach his first sermon in Spanish. I realized that Michael was strongly getting confirmation from God that He wanted him

The kids didn't want Samuel to leave.

to serve as a missionary in Guatemala with E3 Volunteers. The beautiful part about Michael's call was that, at the same time, God was calling Anna to serve in Guatemala, too. They met on that month-long mission trip and soon fell in love. In the future, they plan to serve together as husband and wife in Guatemala. Again my *But God?* became *But God!* I realized once again the perfect plan for my life that God had worked out so long ago.

*O LORD, I will honor and praise your name,
for you are my God.
You do such wonderful things! You planned them long ago,
and now you have accomplished them.*

Isaiah 25:1

Michael and Anna in Antigua

Michael preaching in Spanish for the 1st time

Morgan Hatcher was so loved by all the little children

Sweet Anna playing with the little children

Elayna, Michael, and Samuel playing with the kids

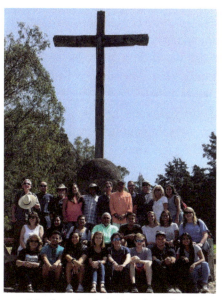

It's about the Cross; it's always been about the Cross.

Chapter 42

On most mission trips, there are difficult days, and you are called on to be flexible. I've always thought I could handle anything, but on the third week of that trip, I felt helpless and afraid. The original team we were supposed to be with had to cancel, so the students and I were the team. I don't think I was prepared for what happened on the way to our mission point.

Samuel got very sick, and he fainted at one of our stops. He was dehydrated and had to be taken to two different rural hospitals for fluids. I was worried, but I quickly learned that God was taking care of him. He provided a close hospital off the highway and even a doctor we knew who lived in the town where we were staying. And God had already given us Kevin, our wonderful coordinator, who carried Samuel on his back when he was too weak to walk. He also gave us Damaris, who lovingly made sure Samuel was taken care of.

Pedialyte, the perfect gift for Samuel's 17th birthday!

A couple of days later, the team surprised Samuel on his 17th birthday with firecrackers, a cake, a piñata, and gifts of Pedialyte. The look on Samuel's face was priceless. That party was beautiful and unforgettable. According to Samuel, it was the best birthday ever.

I don't think I could be any prouder of those students than I was that week. On short notice, they planned an amazing week for the school they worked in. They even purchased their own sports equipment and planned

beautiful worship times and Bible stories. Sadly, some of the other team members got sick, but they all worked hard to make it an unforgettable experience.

114

Samuel, miracle child, was literally made in Guatemala

As a grandmother, I got to experience the most precious sight one day when, while riding in the van, I looked behind me to check on Samuel. He looked so sick and pitiful, but he had his Bible open and was reading it. At that moment, I knew that God was with us and would never leave us. And, I couldn't even imagine it then, *But God* had planned some unbelievable experiences for us in the days ahead.

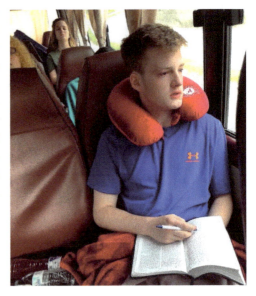

Chapter 43

I was reminded on that month-long trip that the best things in life happen when you don't plan them, *But God* does. Our team and I were in Antigua and had met up with Garry while we were waiting for our last volunteer team to arrive. Garry took us out to eat at Mono Loco, a local restaurant.

While we were eating, we exchanged greetings with a Guatemalan family beside us. Before we finished, Garry told me he felt like the Lord wanted him to pay for their meal. As we were leaving, they found out and ran out to thank him. Garry told Carlos, the father, that he knew they weren't poor, but he felt God had told him to do it anyway—so he did, not really knowing why. We then left and headed to the cathedral at the square to show our group some ruins.

When we arrived, Carlos and his family came up behind us. He approached Garry and told him that his family was going through a difficult time, and they felt that Garry's generosity reassured them that God was with them. Garry then asked them if they could go inside the Catholic church and let him pray for them. The students and I sat behind them and prayed also, but we had no idea what was going on. The entire time Carlos' wife was in tears. Garry and Carlos exchanged numbers, and we left.

Garry joined the group on our free day in Antigua

At Hotel Antigua standing in the exact spot where their dads graduated from high school

Later that evening, Carlos texted Garry and told him the reason they had gone to the church earlier in the day; his wife's parents were in great danger, were being threatened in another town, and they needed to get out as soon as possible. A paramilitary group was going in to get them the next day, and he asked us to pray for their safety and protection. All of us began to pray.

Two days later, we heard from Carlos again. His family had been taken to safety! He was so grateful for our encounter and was so sure that God had used us to reveal to him and his family that He loved them and was with them. Only God can work like that. Only God.

Chapter 44

Look! I stand at the door and knock. If you hear my voice and open the door, I will come in, and we will share a meal together as friends. Those who are victorious will sit with me on my throne, just as I was victorious and sat with my Father on his throne.

Revelation 3:20-21

That "God Appointment" with Carlos was indeed amazing, *But God* had another one for us the next day. On that day, we just wanted to be tourists, and I wanted to take hundreds of pictures of those beautiful young people at one of my favorite places. That's when we met Chris.

I had noticed a group of people close to us, and I asked if anyone could take our picture. Chris spoke up, "I will!" in English, which was very odd because I had asked in Spanish. We found out that he lived in Los Angeles and was visiting family.

After he took our picture, we began to get to know him and learned that he really was not interested in religion. That's when Michael told Chris that it wasn't about religion but a relationship with Jesus. He told him, "Chris, as Jesus was on the cross, He was thinking about you!" Then all the group began talking to Chris and encouraging him and helping him understand that he needed Jesus in his life.

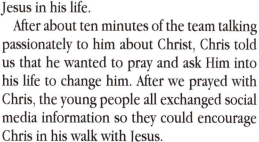

After about ten minutes of the team talking passionately to him about Christ, Chris told us that he wanted to pray and ask Him into his life to change him. After we prayed with Chris, the young people all exchanged social media information so they could encourage Chris in his walk with Jesus.

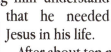
At breakfast before we met Chris

The beautiful thing about this God story is that during breakfast that morning, Garry had shared with us that we shouldn't waste a single opportunity the Lord gives us, and we need to live every moment for Him. I'm thinking that Chris is eternally grateful that we didn't waste that opportunity. His life was changed, but so was ours. We knew we would never be the same.

Michael and his little friend Juan

The team gathered around Chris

Michael and Samuel looking over Lake Atitlan

Samuel, Jon, and Michael standing over Antigua

Headed home after an amazing month in Guatemala

[14]But how can they call on him to save them unless they believe in him? And how can they believe in him if they have never heard about him? And how can they hear about him unless someone tells them? [15]And how will anyone go and tell them without being sent? That is why the Scriptures say, "How beautiful are the feet of messengers who bring good news!"

Romans 10:14-15

Everybody loves McDonald's in Antigua, Guatemala

Samuel and his little friend

As the sun was setting, Fuego was erupting, and God showed me a cross in the clouds of smoke.

Chapter 45

One thing I know for sure: our lives have never been boring. We've lived, loved, and often laughed until we've cried. The older we get, the more fun we have. And it's never-ending.

One day, Garry took me to the grocery store and stayed in the car while I picked up a few things. He was on the phone when I finished, but he got off and put the groceries in the car for me. We headed home and, on our way there, he said, "Where is my phone?" He stopped and searched everywhere in the car. Then, "Oh no! I hope I didn't put it on top of the car and drive off!" I decided to call his phone just in case it had fallen in between the seats. I called. It rang and rang on my phone. No sound—nothing. Then suddenly, I felt this vibration on my booty. Yes! I absolutely was sitting on his phone and didn't know it. Panic turned into relief and hysterical laughter!

Sometimes, even with a phone, those conversations can be challenging. Every night whenever Garry is in Guatemala, he calls me to talk before we go to sleep. He asked me once what I was going to do the next day. I told him, "I'm going to have a smashing good time having a mammogram." His response, "So, you're going to have a good time running around? Where are you going to run around at?"

Because of our work, we get to visit churches and attend various meetings. One time we arrived in Nashville, Tennessee, to attend the annual convention of the

122

Tennessee Baptist Mission Board. At the hotel, we were given a key to our room, but when we opened the door, a man was sitting on top of the bed in his underwear and socks watching a football game. Well, hello. We didn't stick around to find out the score of that game.

Once we were in Sevierville, Tennessee, and Garry had preached a powerful missions sermon at First Baptist Church, Sevierville. I jokingly said to him that I was surprised he could put two thoughts together at his age. As we headed home from that trip, I asked him where his coffee was. "Oops, I think I left it in the trunk!"

Another time we were in Pigeon Forge celebrating our anniversary. We were in an outlet store, shopping. Garry walked up to a lady from behind, and thinking he was talking to me, asked her if she needed socks. She turned around, stared at him, and moved away from him as fast as she could.

At our age, we don't babysit children anymore, but we do quite a bit of dog sitting for our kids and grandkids. On one of those occasions Garry had just come in from walking one of the dogs and rushed into the bathroom while I was taking a shower. "I thought I was going to have to make like a dog and use one of the shrubs myself!" I told him that he'd better not or someone would call the police on him. Then he said, "Well, maybe when I'm eighty years old, I might get away with it. Do you think I'll live until I'm eighty?" "I hope so," I said. Then, knowing that I don't like it when he flushes the toilet when I'm in the shower, he said, "I bet if I flush this toilet, I won't live till I'm eighty!" Me, "Nope, you won't!" Oh, we were laughing all the way through that one!

Yep. That's my main man, best-ever preacher man, missionary man, mountain man, sports car driving man, jeep loving man, best friend, and love of my life. He's still the one, and we're still having fun! I just love doing life with him!

Chapter 46

As the sun was setting on 2018, our family traveled together to the beautiful country of Panama, where our mission experiences first began. It's impossible to describe the feelings I had going back to Panama with our family. What I can say is that I'm so thankful God called us to serve Him there so many years ago.

Our grandkids loved seeing where their parents had grown up. We went from a high-rise hotel in the city to the Gamboa Rainforest, to the Panama Canal, to the beach, and then on to the mountain town of Boquete. Our boys acted like monkeys swinging from trees; we saw real monkeys; we watched ships pass through the Canal; we rode aerial trams above the jungle; rode horses on the beach; ate delicious Panamanian cuisine; saw majestic scenery; hiked to hidden waterfalls; zip-lined; and visited with precious old friends. It was for sure the most perfect family vacation ever!

The grandkids gathered around Garry as he explained how the Panama Canal locks work

But wait! On second thought, nothing is as perfect as it seems. Grant got a speeding ticket. We didn't have water at our beach house all day on January 1st, and Rob hauled water from the ocean to the house to flush toilets. On that same day, Grant found some Preparation H wipes and washed his hands with them. He said, "Well, at least my hands won't swell today!"

Somebody didn't think about taking toilet paper on our three-hour hike up

Grant swinging from a tree like when he was a kid

125

the mountain, so we had to use paper towels. There was no door on the outside of that rustic mountain bathroom, but I sure had a beautiful view as I sat there.

Garry dreamed that he had been arrested and woke up in jail for not paying taxes when we lived in Panama. Michael was dreaming when he woke up that he was giving a devotional, and he came across a verse that said, *Get up, therefore, and go pee*. So, he did.

Of course, nothing is ever perfect. *But God* gave our family a perfectly wonderful, unforgettable experience together in Panama, planned by the best of the best, our daughter Christen.

Kaylee guarding the outside bathroom for me, ready with the paper towels – what a view from the potty!

Garry and I loved our Boquete coffee

Riding horses

Beautiful sunrise from our beach house

Hiking the mountain trail outside Boquete

Panama Canal view from the jungle

Hotel at the Gamboa Rainforest

Hotel in Boquete

Chapter 47

On February 18, 2019, a Facebook Memory reminded me of an event that I could never forget. Exactly three years before, in 2016, literally thousands of people all over the world were praying for Kayla's healing from cancer. As I shared earlier, her doctors had told her family that she had only six to eight weeks to live. We never thought she would live to marry Austin, much less have more time on this earth. *But God* gave us the most incredible miracle! Three years had passed, and Kayla was still with us! Kayla and Austin celebrated their third anniversary in May 2019! For me, it's still unbelievable. Every single day we have with her is a miracle.

Kayla at Answer to Cancer

Kayla has been passionately working with her organization, Open Hands Overflowing Hearts, to raise awareness and funds to find a cure for childhood cancer. She sponsors events like Answer to Cancer and Run for Their Lives every year. She has, at this point, raised $2,000,000.00! She's also making a difference in the personal lives of children with cancer. She visits the children and their families and lets them tell

Kayla with her dad at Answer to Cancer

Gold Gala sponsored by Open Hands Overflowing Hearts

Gold Gala with Morgan and Kayla

At Gold Gala with our sons Grant and Greg

their stories. Using her amazing photography skills, she gives the families beautiful photos of their children. The families of these children know that Kayla is working hard advocating for them. God is definitely still writing her story!

Christen, Kayla's mom, recently wrote again about her early struggles during Kayla's battle with cancer. She spent many days and nights crying out to God, screaming and begging Him for miracles and Kayla's healing. She quoted this on August 17, 2016. "And, if I didn't believe this, with all my heart, I might not make it out of bed some days: what is coming will make sense of what is happening. Let God finish His work. Let the Composer complete His symphony. The forecast is simple. Good days. Bad days. *But God* is in All days. He is the Lord of the famine and the feast, and He uses both to accomplish His will."

Believing that God is still in ALL days, Christen wrote this in 2019: "God was in those days—the feast and the famine—the good ones and the bad ones. He used ALL those days to accomplish His will. He is still working." Yes, He definitely is.

> *Your display of wonders, miracles, and power makes the nations acknowledge you.*
> Psalms 77:14 (TPT)

Gold balloon release before Run for Their Lives

Kayla emcees at Run for Their Lives 5K Event

The family at Run for Their Lives

Kayla uses Photography to support Kids with Cancer

Kayla Update 2021

*Kayla is in her fifth year of living with
"No Evidence of Disease."
She's a living, walking miracle.
Kayla and Austin celebrated their
5th wedding anniversary
on May 21st, 2021.
Our family is grateful
every day for her extraordinary life.*

Chapter 48

I know from living life that not all things are good, but I also know that God works in all things. In 2019 we needed God's peace and comfort as we experienced some very difficult days. Garry and I unexpectedly lost two very special people in our lives.

One was a precious dear friend, a former church member, who, even after we left, let us know that Garry would always be her favorite pastor. We were devastated when we learned of Brenda's untimely death. (She was my friend who saved me, "her pastor's wife," from getting a speeding ticket.) Brenda always told us that Jesus was her best friend, and I believed it. Heaven is a sweeter place because she is there.

Garry Baptizing Brenda in the Jordon River

We also lost my sister's husband Doug. He loved to decorate the house for Christmas. While on the roof, tragically, he fell to his death. He and Garry were great friends. They could talk sports and history for hours without stopping while my sister Ann Marie and I were out shopping without stopping!

In March of 2019, when I knew my sister and Doug were coming for a visit, I asked Garry, "Do you think while they are here, we can go to Tuscaloosa?" Garry responded, "No, I don't think we can go to Costa Rica!" We did, however, spend a day in Tuscaloosa visiting the campus of the University of Alabama. We walked all over, talking, laughing, making new memories, and reminiscing about our years there. Doug didn't stop smiling all day. It was one of our most special times together and, sadly, it was the last time we saw him. At Doug's celebration of life service, his beautiful grandchildren all talked about their special relationship with him. They obviously loved him so dearly because of his endless generosity and time spent with each of them. They all made him so proud! It was such a hard goodbye, and all of us miss him so very much. We're so thankful that one day we will see him again!

Losing a loved one is so very hard, *But God* is close to the brokenhearted and is ever-present with those of us who are grieving. He holds us in His Loving Arms, and we are never alone.

Ann Marie with her beautiful children and grandchildren after Doug's Celebration of Life Service

Chapter 49

Life often brings tears and mourning, but it also brings many special moments to celebrate. In 2019, Garry and I got to experience many of those life moments.

As blessed grandparents of eight, it seemed we were always celebrating something. Morgan graduated from Auburn University, and several months later, Cameron asked her to marry him. Our Andrew is now serving our country in the U.S. Air Force as an air traffic control specialist. Garry and I got to attend his graduation from air traffic control technical training school. After graduation, he and his spouse Nathan moved to Hill Air Force Base in Salt Lake City, where Andrew is now a senior airman. Both Samuel and Michael graduated from high school and started college. We got to watch our extremely musically talented Daniel perform in his high school's jazz band, the Symphonic Winds, and the marching band. Jared, who has the fastest legs ever, excited us as he ran track and cross country. Our Kaylee, our amazing champion gymnast, is always so much fun to watch!

We are so very proud of all our grandchildren. We love them so much!

As a couple, Garry and I celebrated 50 years of marriage in 2019! We celebrated all year, every moment we could. Our ultimate celebration happened in October when we cruised from

Barcelona, Spain, to Monaco, France, Italy, Greece, Croatia, and back to Italy. It was the trip of a lifetime for us, especially since we never had a honeymoon. We will forever be grateful to God for putting us together, my parents for their generosity, Christen for planning the trip, and our kids for making it possible for us to extend our trip from Venice to Florence and back to Rome by train. It seemed unbelievable to think that, 50 years before, we had started out in an old, ugly trailer. I never could have imagined experiencing something so incredibly beautiful. *But God* is the endless Giver of blessings.

2019 was also a stellar year for E3 Volunteers. Seventy-five teams from the States went to Guatemala to minister! For the first time, we had a full-time missionary, Jon, living and working at our seminary. We also had four full-time national missionaries: Kevin, Director of Mobilization, Raquel, Financial Administrator, Maricarmen, Seminary Administrator, and Damaris, Director of Family Ministries. David, one of our faithful volunteers from Tennessee, felt God leading him to join our staff, and he became our U.S. Director of Mobilization and Financial Administrator. Our grandson Michael joined

the staff and became our Director of Media and Communications.

At the end of 2019, we, along with our staff, our mobilizers, and their families, had a prayer and planning retreat in Guatemala. We prayed and planned for at least 100 teams in 2020. And to think that Garry, with the help of translators in Guatemala, started out in 2011 by taking four teams by himself. Nobody could have ever imagined. *But God* knew, and He had planned it long ago. We couldn't wait to see what He was about to do in 2020.

Chapter 50

Raise your hand if you wish we could have a do-over of 2020. Mine is raised. I think maybe the only people who really had a good year were those in the mask and toilet paper-making business.

Our year began in a fairly normal way. Garry and I were given adult tricycles for Christmas and having the time of our lives riding through our neighborhood. During one of those rides, I told Garry that if I died before he did I knew he would be fine by himself, and there would be no need for him to look for someone to take my place. He looked over at me and said, "Don't worry Honey. I won't ever let another woman ride your trike." "Good answer," I told him. We got home from that ride, and he told me, "Okay, I'm ready to watch a Hallmark Movie with you now." I said, "I'm so proud of you!" He looked sadly at me and asked, "Why are you tired of me?"

I found a Dr Pepper in Antigua, Guatemala!

With Ingrid and Otto, the beautiful friends who prayed with us the night my mom went to be with Jesus

In early March, we made a trip to Guatemala for a retreat for our pastors and their wives. I was privileged to share a study with the pastors' wives about loving God and loving others, a subject that is my greatest desire. I want to love God more than anything and love others more than I love myself.

I came home from that trip, took off my jewelry, and didn't wear it for the rest of the year. I did spend about five minutes one morning trying to put a bangle bracelet in my earlobe, thinking it was my earring! I thought the hole was closed since I had not worn earrings for so long!

During 2020 I cut my own hair, rescued my own roots, and took care of my own fingernails while Garry lovingly trimmed my toenails. I didn't even use a tenth of the clothes, shoes, and purses I own. I didn't go to the mall, but I must admit that I did some online shopping where I purchased some of the cutest masks. They matched some of the clothes I wasn't wearing. Life in 2020 was like nothing I had ever experienced.

With Kevin and fiancé Katarina who met while she was a Semester Missionary with E3

Pastors who were led in a leadership study by Pastor Stephen Peeples

These beautiful pastors' wives were such fun to be with; I loved my time with them.

Chapter 51

Who could have ever imagined what 2020 would be like? Covid was the word most spoken in the world. It literally changed every aspect of our lives. It changed the way we lived, how we behaved, where we went, and even how we felt. For me, it was one time I needed to trust God's plan even though I could not understand or see the path before me.

We experienced one of our biggest disappointments as a family: Morgan and Cameron had planned their dream wedding at Disney World for May 3rd; sadly, that didn't happen. They got married in a small, private ceremony in April. Morgan wrote this afterward: "This pandemic has presented us with indescribable amounts of difficulty, but we are thankful that the Lord is teaching us humility and trust during this season of life. We are choosing to believe that

He's not taking away our most beloved ceremonies and celebrations, but that He is sculpting His children to see beyond the activities of this world and into the Heart of our One true Savior! We are immeasurably blessed and thankful." Morgan's words profoundly affected me, and as I look back on 2020, I realize what a loving heart my Jesus has.

Because of Covid-closed borders, we knew that Guatemala would not be receiving the one hundred teams that we had planned for. *But God?* Soon, we learned that many people were suffering and were hungry there. What were we to do? We couldn't go! *But God* answered our prayers for the people! First Baptist Church, Hendersonville, Tennessee, sent money to feed five thousand people and eventually fed ten thousand. Other partners also responded to the need, and we were eventually able to feed ten thousand more throughout the country. I doubt, even if we had gone, we'd have been able to touch that many people. Plus, as our churches in Guatemala gave out the food baskets, they were able to share Christ's love. Hundreds came to know Him because someone cared enough to give, go in the name of Jesus, and meet the physical needs of the people.

1 John 3:17-18 became so real to me: *But if anyone has the world's goods and sees his brother in need, yet closes his heart against him, how does God's love abide in him? Little children, let us not love in word or talk, but in deed and in truth.*

We quickly learned that if you can't go, you love as you *Zoom*. What? Zooming became a very popular thing at our house. Garry was able to keep in touch with his staff

Salvador Zapeta, President of the Guatemala Baptist Convention, helped in the COVID19 Relief Effort.

Pastor Luis Avila distributing food to the firemen. Sadly, we lost Luis to COVID19 later in 2021.

and mobilizers every week. They shared, prayed, and studied the Bible together. I loved watching and listening during those Zoom calls, but I tried to hide when I was not ready to be seen. Sometimes, however, they saw me anyway, and if they didn't, Garry would hear me and say, "Come and say hello to everybody, Kathy!"

It was exciting to listen to their meetings and conversations about future goals. E3 Volunteers will begin to take teams to Honduras and Costa Rica in 2021 and, of course, continue going to Guatemala. In

2020 also brought hurricanes and flooding into Alta Verapaz and Itzabal, Guatemala

January 2021, Anna, Michael's future wife, arrived in Guatemala as a full-time missionary to set up programs for teaching English in partner churches and schools. Her goal is to share Christ as she teaches. Michael hopes that one day, E3 Volunteers will be a global organization. He's already been to Kenya and Greece and hopes to go back. I may not live to see it, *But God* can do it! E3 Volunteers' motto is, "Whatever He says, *Do*. Whenever He says, *Move*. Wherever He says, *Go*. We will obey!"

*Be still and know that I am God! I will be honored by every nation.
I will be honored throughout the world.*

Psalm 46:10

Chapter 52

I would never want to be dismissive of the tragic events in 2020. Covid, sickness, death, social unrest, violence, joblessness, hatred, divisiveness, hurricanes, wildfires, and floods affected so many of us. Never have I experienced so many negative emotions in one year. I was sad, heartbroken, angry, afraid, and confused.

In June, we found out that Garry had some blockages in his heart. The truth is that if he had been in Guatemala, as he planned to be, he quite possibly could have had a heart attack and died. *But God* did not allow that to happen. Garry did, however, have to wait for open-heart surgery until July because of the rise in Covid cases being treated in the hospital.

The wait was hard and became unbearable, because during that time, we had to say goodbye to our precious little 16-year-old dog Blanca, and our beautiful

12-year-old black cat Buddy. We were heartbroken over the loss of our little family members. Their love was special to us because it was truly unconditional. I don't think I've cried as much in my whole life as I cried during those days and weeks after their deaths. In fact, I still cry when I think about the good times, the memories, the happiness, the laughs, and the comfort they gave us down through the years. Our hearts are still healing from the loss.

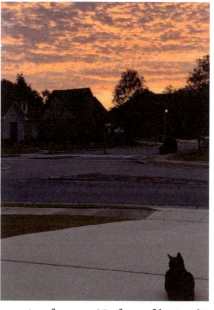

A couple of weeks before Garry's surgery, I was beginning to get anxious. I asked him after we got into bed one night if he was scared. He told me that he was not. Then I began to cry and said, "Well, I'm scared." He didn't judge me. He just lovingly took my hand and started praying for me. My fear of losing him was real, *But God* has always been faithful, and all I knew to do was trust Him.

Don't worry about anything; instead, pray about everything.
Tell God what you need and thank him for all he has done.
Philippians 4:6

Chapter 53

The day of the surgery and the weeks that followed were some of the most difficult times of my life. We left home early on the day of the surgery and took the scenic route to the hospital. We have so many memories on that road and got to relive some. Plus, God let us see the most beautiful sunrise.

For me, the wait at the hospital was almost unbearable. I ate a peanut butter and banana sandwich that Garry had made me before we left home, and then I kissed him so he could have a little taste since he wasn't supposed to eat before surgery. While we waited together, we had some sweet private moments. My heart skipped a beat when tears appeared in those beautiful blue eyes of his. When they took him away, I was crying. *But God* let me feel His Presence and Peace. I was even confident that God would be with him, because as one friend said to him, "You have all the western hemisphere praying for you!" It seemed like the surgery took forever. I even had time to go home and give myself a "Covid" haircut, all while praying and believing that Garry was going to make it through his surgery.

When the surgery was finally over six hours later, the surgeon came out and told our sons and me that he had hit a home run— a triple bypass and an ablation. The doctor was positive he would make a complete recovery! It was hard for me, however, when I saw Garry in CICU with all the tubes and wires. When the nurse removed his ventilator, I told him I loved him. He whispered softly, "I love you, too." Those words were the sweetest words I had heard all day.

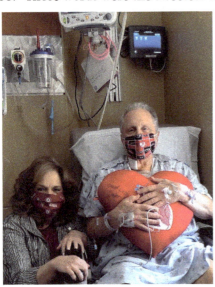

I was told that recovery from open-heart surgery is more like a marathon than a sprint, but I had never seen anybody more determined to recover than Garry. Even his occupational therapist couldn't believe it when, the day after surgery, he did everything she asked him to. Then she asked him, "What else can you do?" He might have been on a few pain meds when he answered, "I can dance!" So the preacher and the therapist danced! I might have taken more than a few pictures.

Because of Covid, no one could visit Garry but Greg and me, so it was the most precious surprise when our kids and grandkids showed up outside of his hospital window waving their arms and holding signs of love and encouragement for healing. One of the signs was Isaiah 58:11, *The Lord will guide you always*. The other was Psalm 57:7-9, *My Heart is steadfast, Oh God, my Heart is steadfast. I will sing, yes, I will sing praises. Awake harp and lyre! I will awaken the dawn. I will give thanks to You, Oh Lord, among the peoples. I will sing praises to You*

among the nations! Of course, "We love you, Tito" was the sweetest sign ever. It was a perfect socially distanced get well party! There may have been a few tears.

My health may fail, and my spirit may grow weak, But God remains the strength of my heart; he is mine forever.

Psalms 73:26

Don't be afraid, for I am with you.
Don't be discouraged, for I am your God.
I will strengthen you and help you.
I will hold you up with
my victorious right hand.

Isaiah 41:10

Chapter 54

So how do you survive your new normal in abnormal conditions? I know one thing; we couldn't have survived without the Lord, our family, and loving friends. Covid was on the move, and Garry's baby heart did not allow us to leave the house. There were lots of mask-wearing, socially distanced front porch visits with our kids, grandkids, and friends. They brought meals and gave us numerous virtual hugs. Some even brought get-well baskets full of goodies for us to enjoy. We became friends with the sweet girl who delivered our groceries, and we now are forever friends.

When you can't go to church, you "livestream!" God used First Baptist Church Hendersonville, Tennessee, to minister to us every Sunday. They not only fed thousands of Guatemalans in 2020, but their pastor Dr. Bruce Chesser, fed us spiritually throughout the year. His messages and the worship moments were just what we needed.

Our kids made sure we didn't go out anywhere in public places, so we might have been a little crazier than we already were. We were seriously trying to eat more healthy foods, so for lunch one day, we were making a salad with smoked chicken on top. I told Garry, "The chicken is heating up, and it's already deboned." His response: "Oh, no! It's already burned up?" Then on another morning, Garry said, "Could you please call my phone? I can't find it." Later on, I told him, "I have no idea where I put my coffee." Garry: "Too bad you can't call it and find it." If we asked each other what day it was one time, we asked it a thousand times during that year. It was a different life, *But God* blessed us with Garry's recovery and good health. He is a Good, Good Father!

Chapter 55

How do you make sense of all the trials that 2020 brought? It also seemed that 2020 went out and put on a mask and came back as 2021! I don't claim to have 20/20 vision, but I do know a few things that God taught me. I didn't think I was ready to take it on, *But God* had been preparing me all through my life to keep walking with Him and trusting Him. He is always in control. And, as always, I could see God working in our lives and our ministry in ways we could not have ever imagined before.

I must say that for Garry and me personally, that year was the most unusual of our lives together. Never had we spent 365 days, 24 hours a day, and 7 days a week in the same space. We definitely had some adjusting to do. Because we are flawed, not all the days were problem free. Many times, we had to ask for forgiveness and forgive each other for things we said or did. I can truthfully say, though, that there's no one else I'd rather grow old with than him. He knows me so well, and he gets me even though he might not hear every word I say! On Valentine's Day, he went out and picked up lunch at one of my favorite places. We sat down to eat, and he turned on his playlist of love songs. He looked over at me and sang a phrase or a line of each song. Then he smiled and winked at me. After we finished lunch, we got up and danced together to the song, *I Will Always Love You*. I just fell in love with him all over again! No, we're not special or perfect, *But God* gave us each other to love and cherish in whatever circumstances we find ourselves until we die. And we will.

At times it was so hard to be happy when everything seemed to be going wrong, *But God* didn't promise me a perfect life with no trials. He did, however, promise to be with me and give me strength for whatever I'm facing. God doesn't want me to pursue happiness but to choose Joy and Contentment in all my circumstances. I'll admit that I've always struggled with fear and worry, *But God* has always been my Help and my Comforter and my Peace.

So, as always, if I'm truly looking for what really mattered in 2020 and what matters in life, I have to "look into the Heart of my one true Savior," as Morgan so appropriately said. My thoughts go back to when God created man and woman so that He could have a relationship with us. But throughout history, our sins have kept us from really knowing His heart. *But God* loved us so much that He sent His Son, Jesus, to us so that we can truly know Him.

Jesus is Who really matters. And, for me, it matters if I have a relationship with Him or not. It's not about religion. It's about a relationship every day with Jesus. How else can I know God, if not through His Son? He came to earth and showed me how to love everybody, to forgive, to not judge, to comfort and share others' burdens, to serve others, to show tolerance, and to show compassion, mercy, and grace. And, most importantly, He showed me how to follow God's will by going to the cross and dying a horrible death so I might be forgiven of all my sins. What a Savior! Who else can change my heart? Only Jesus. He alone is the answer for me, my broken country, and my world. He defines me. I choose Him. Every. Time. No one ever changed the world with anger, hatred, and violence. *But God*'s love changes everything.

For this is how God loved the world: He gave his one and only Son, so that everyone who believes in him will not perish but have eternal life.

John 3:16

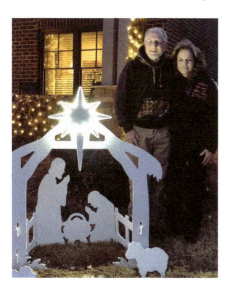

Chapter 56

The older I get, the more I think about dying. Will I leave a legacy? After a couple of generations, will anyone even remember me? Will they care that I loved hats and shoes and purses? Will they even know that I loved to decorate early for Christmas? Will they care that I'm a dog kisser and, yes, a cat lover? Will it matter that I was a preacher's wife and a missionary and went to church every Sunday? Will it matter what my houses were like or what kinds of cars I've driven? Will they even care where in the world I've traveled? Will anyone on earth ever care about the things I've collected or the thousands of photos I've  taken? Will anyone know what football team I pulled for or who I voted for in 2020? I'm just going to go ahead and answer "NO!" to all those questions.

I do, however, know WHO will be remembered. I read something when I was a kid that has stuck with me my entire life. It said, "Only one life; it will soon be past. Only what's done for Christ will last." I would say that it won't be what I've done for Christ that will last, but what Christ did for me. Life is about Him, and, yes, how I've responded to Him. Have I loved God with all my heart, soul, and  mind and loved others more than I love my selfish self like Jesus told me to do? Will my world be a better place because I've loved everybody, even the unlovely? Have I loved enough to share Jesus with those who don't know Him? Do my actions show that I love? Do I put on love every day? I can answer those questions, too. No, I haven't loved with a perfect love. I've struggled, and I've failed so many times. But I know that I want my life and all I've experienced during my life to point to Him, the One who loved perfectly. *Observe how Christ loved us. His love was not cautious, but extravagant. He didn't love in order to get something from us, but to give everything of Himself to us. Love like that.* Ephesians 5:2. No, my name will not be remembered, but the Name of Jesus will.

Yes, as I grow old, my health may fail, and my mind may grow weak, *But God* will always be my Strength, my Comfort, my Help, My Guide, my Provider, my Healer, my Protector, my Defender, my Teacher, and my Hope. Nothing can separate me from His Love. I love Him. I praise Him. I thank Him for the plan He had for me so long ago. I give Him all the glory for everything He has done during my lifetime. And I'm so very grateful that He allowed me to watch Him work. Truly, it's been a beautiful and exciting journey! One day I will see Him face to face and will live forever and ever with my Creator, my Loving Father.

For ever since the world was created, people have seen the earth and sky. Through everything God made, they can clearly see his invisible qualities—his eternal power and divine nature. So they have no excuse for not knowing God.

Romans 1:20

I want my life and all that I've experienced during my life to point to Him, the One who loved perfectly.

Watch what God does, *and then you do it, like children who learn proper behavior from their parents.* ***Mostly what God does is love you.*** *Keep company with him and learn a life of love.* ***Observe how Christ loved us.*** *His love was not cautious but extravagant. He didn't love in order to get something from us but to give everything of himself to us.* ***Love like that.***

Ephesians 5:1-2 MSG

Addendum

In May, 2021, Garry, along with his staff of E3 Volunteers and Kevin Williams, Pastor of FBC Villa Rica, Georgia planned and hosted a historical summit in the country of Costa Rica. Baptist leaders from Guatemala, Costa Rica, Honduras, El Salvador, Nicaragua and Panamá gathered there with leaders from Georgia, Alabama and Tennessee. They sought ways, using volunteers, to help reach the ones in Central America who don't know Jesus. As a result of this summit, thousands will come to know Him. For some, this is hard to believe, *But God* had this planned long, long ago. We give Him all the glory! He's still working!

CPSIA information can be obtained
at www.ICGtesting.com
Printed in the USA
LVHW071145310721
694127LV00010BA/334